Whatever Remembers Us:
An Anthology of Alabama Poetry

"Whatever remembers us, finally, is enough.
If anything remembers, something is love."

— John Ciardi, "Minus One"

Edited by
Sue Brannan Walker
and
J. William Chambers

Negative Capability Press
Mobile, Alabama

Whatever Remembers Us:
An Anthology of Alabama Poetry

Copyright 2007
Negative Capability Press

All rights reserved

ISBNs: 978-0-942544-60-2 (Paperback)
 978-0-942544-62-6 (Hardback)

Library of Congress Control Number: 2007902971

Cover Photographs by Jason R. Walker:
 Alabama Shakespeare Theatre
 Alabama State Capitol

Cover Design by Megan Cary

Negative Capability Press
Mobile, Alabama

Contents

I. Places Remember

Bruce Alford
    Rappelling at Eagle's Point / 3
Jerri Beck
    Driving to Montgomery / 4
Jack Bedell
    My Son Discovers the Draw of Water / 6
T. J. Beitelman
    The World Peace Poem / 7
Margaret Key Biggs
    The Rattling of Bones / 9
Jeff Blake
    My Alabama Home / 10
Ray Bradbury
    Poem Written On a Train Just Leaving a Small Southern Town / 12
Joanne Ramey Cage
    Red Clay Poet / 14
Mark Dawson
    Lunch with Kelley at the Montgomery Museum of Fine Arts Café M / 15
Tom Drinkard
    The Post Office / 16
Deborah Ferguson
    While Driving Through Alabama's Black Belt / 21
John Finlay
    The Road to the Gulf / 22
Abby Frierson
    Alabama Vistas / 23
Maurice Gandy
    Church Street Cemetery: Mobile, Alabama / 24
Virginia Gilbert
    The Casting of Lots / 25
Andrew Glaze
    Red Mountain / 27

John Halbrooks
    Exeter Book Riddle 8:
    A Gulf-Coast Paraphrase / 28
Andrew Hudgins
    Ashes / 29
J. P. Jones
    Remembering Alabama
    from Japan / 30
Willie James King
    Old Cahawba / 31
Thomas Lakeman
    Driving On Through
    Foley, Alabama / 32
Irene Latham
    The Quilts of Gee's Bend / 34
Celia Vickery Lewis
    Canoe, Alabama, 1961 / 35
Carey Link
    My Alabama Home / 36
Susan Luther
    Two Views of Howard's Chapel / 37
James Mersmann
    Chilton County Woods:
    Revisiting the Garden in Ruins / 39
William Miller
    The Moon in Delta, Alabama / 41
Mary Murphy
    Mostly Home / 43
Susan Murphy
    Who D'Ya Pull For? / 45
Helen Norris
    Capitol City Yesteryear / 47
Phyllis Peck
    Musings from a Small
    Alabama Town / 48
Georgette Perry
    Montgomery, 1922 / 49
Marge Piercy
    Becoming mobile in Mobile / 51
Thomas Rabbitt
    After the Flood / 52
Tut Riddick
    Spirit Square: York, Alabama / 53

Sue Scalf
> Montgomery, 1990 / 54

Eric Smith
> Cotton's Pond, 1982 / 56

Marilyn Tarvin
> Cotton and Calculus / 57

Donna Jean Tennis
> Home from the Hunt / 58

Jeanie Thompson
> At Moundville / 61

Doris Gabel Welch
> My South / 63

Rob Whitaker
> A Porch; Pine Hill, Alabama / 65

Isabelle Whitman
> Lateral Movement / 66

Joseph Whitten
> Climbing Sand Mountain / 67

Miller Williams
> Plain / 68

II. People Remember

Gerald Barrax
> Why I am Jerald with a G and Gerry with a J / 71

Frederick W. Bassett
> A Dollhouse / 72

Alexis Beard
> All That I Am / 73

Allen Berry
> The Agrarian / 74

Richard G. Beyer
> To Marjorie . . . Nine Years Gone / 75

Jon Carter
> Driving After Trying To Reach You, Paul / 77

Caitlin Channell
> Old Men Chew Canned Tobacco and Call it Tasty / 79

John Curbow
    Father and Son / 80
Rita Dove
    Rosa / 81
Frances R. Durham
    Fishermen at Fairhope / 82
Vernon Fowlkes
    The Peach Speaks To Helen Gill:
    Bickford Station, AL, 1899 / 83
Diane Garden
    Portrait of My Father and Me
    with the USS Alabama / 85
Faye Gaston
    War Widow, 1863 / 86
Gail Gehlken
    Alabama women / 87
Anne George
    This Day I Give My Father / 88
Mary Halliburton
    The Legacy / 89
Ralph Hammond
    Molly and Josephus of Upper Alabama / 90
Peter Huggins
    John Beecher in Birmingham / 91
Ramona L. Hyman
    Mind Chatter: For Rosa Parks / 92
Rodney Jones
    Two Girls At The Hartselle, Alabama,
    Municipal Swimming Pool / 95
Penne Laubenthal
    Alabama Clay: Mentone, 1989 / 96
Karen Middleton
    The Snow of '88 / 97
Claire W. Mikkelsen
    Soul Brothers? / 98
Shayla Mollohan
    Enough: The Wake You Wanted,
    Lake Guntersville, 1993 / 99
Carl Morton
    To a Neighbor Who Knew / 101
Cheryl Moyer
    The Secret of Old Age / 102

Michael Pollick
    Modern Cuts for Modern Men / 104
David Pratt
    The Gift That's Unexpected / 105
Morton Prouty
    Valedictory / 106
Pat Schneider
    One Day in Mobile / 107
Thomi Sharpe
    Delta's Blues / 108
Jim Simmerman
    Child's Grave, Hale County, Alabama/ 110
Julie Suk
    Whoever They Call Mad / 112
Kathleen Thompson
    Men Going Fishing / 114
Sue Brannan Walker
    The Nature of Dreams:
    The Making of a Naturalist / 116
Jake Adam York
    Walt Whitman in Alabama / 118

III. Music Remembers

Leonard Aldes
    Oh Alabama, I'll Remember You / 123
Jake Berry
    Alabama Dust / 124
Langston Hughes
    Daybreak in Alabama / 126
Hank Lazer
    Banjo / 127
Melissa Morphew
    Alabama Afternoon: A Love Song / 128
John T. Morris
    Rondeau to William Christopher Handy / 129
Richard Scott Nokes
    Bluegrass Bards of Alabama / 130
Jack Pendarvis
    Hank Williams / 132
Margaret Britton Vaughn
    Hank / 133

Eugene Walter
> The Night Concert at Dog River / 134

William J. Wilson
> Old Bookem / 135

C. W. Zoan
> Acrostic Hymn to Huntsville / 136

IV. Seasons Remember

Jane Allen
> Cotton Pickin', 1953 / 139

J. William Chambers
> Farewell to a Garden:
> Athens, Alabama, Autumn 2002 / 140

Reese Danley-Kilgo
> One Alabama Spring / 142

Wade Hall
> A Call to Winter Uses / 143

Juanita Hendrix Holliman
> Thanksgiving 2002 / 145

Reilly Maginn
> Alabama November / 146

Damon Marbut
> the aim of pity / 147

Jim Reed
> One of Those Thanksgiving Days
> in Verbena, Alabama / 148

Julia Rowell
> Blue House in Summer / 149

Abram Ryan
> To the Children of Mary of the
> Cathedral of Mobile / 150

Vivian Smallwood
> Summer Vacation / 151

Claiborne Schley Walsh
> Fall Afternoon / 152

Patti White
> The Wind in Tuscaloosa / 154

Nancy Compton Williams
> Thanksgiving Day in Alabama Foothills / 156

V. Yesterday Remembers

Joe M. Berry
    Yesterday in Alabama / 159
Margaret G. Cutchins
    Green Promise / 162
Walt Darring
    Creek Days / 163
James Dickey
    The Escape / 165
R. Garth
    In Alabama / 167
John Hafner
    Nostalgia / 169
Donna Holt
    Fair Play / 170
Yvonne Kalen
    Wake Up, America / 171
Marjorie Lees Linn
    Outside the Shadows / 172
Susan Martinello
    Night Train / 174
Shelia Smith Mau
    Dried Apples and Cotton Ticking / 175
Samuel Minturn Peck
    The Grapevine Swing / 176
Lora Perry
    Alabama Treasure / 178
Kathleen Petersen
    Reminiscences of Mid-Century Alabama / 179
Bonnie Roberts
    Poems of Mine Readers Cannot Follow / 180
Charles Rodning
    Sense of Place: Sweet Home Alabama / 182
Joseph Sackett
    Ghosts / 185
Sonia Sanchez
    Present / 187
Teresa K. Thorne
    Alabama Dreams in Black and White / 189
Frank X. Walker
    Fireproof / 190

Jamie Yerby
    when we come home or
    moving miles away from nothing / 192

VI. Nature Remembers

Steve Bailey
    An Alabama Night Walk: June 1983 / 197
Robin Behn
    Patton Lake, Tuscaloosa / 198
Patricia Crosby Burchfield
    Freedom of the River / 200
Bettye Kramer Cannizzo
    Dance of the Yellowhammers / 201
Carol Case
    Wildlife Sanctuary / 202
Mary Brobston Cleverdon
    Nesting / 203
A. M. Davis
    This Alabama Earth / 205
Dwight Eddins
    The Tombigbee at Naheola / 207
Charles Ghigna
    The Alabama Elm / 208
Juliana Gray
    Peaches / 209
Theodore Haddin
    How Trees Go Down in Alabama / 210
B. Kim Hagar
    Night Reverie on Elk River / 211
Dennis Hale
    Elba Beware! / 213
Jerri Hardesty
    Night Does Not Fall / 214
Kennette Harrison
    Alabama Afterstorm / 216
Ava Leavell Haymon
    Coelenterata: Gulf Shores, Alabama / 218
Jay Higginbotham
    Bitchina / 219
Evelyn Hurley
    To Alabama / 220

Mary Brunini McArdle
    Alabama Sunset / 221
Tom McDougle
    A Blue-Tailed Lizard on the Porch of
    Alabama's Oldest Wood-Framed House / 222
Jessica McNealy Miles
    Seven Ways to Look at Tiny Minnows / 223
Barry Marks
    Shelby County Coyote / 225
Carter Martin
    Visiting Waterfalls in Bankhead Forest / 227
Mary Carol Moran
    Alabama Dog / 228
Jim Murphy
    Almost Georgic, Alabama / 230
Patricia Sammon
    Alabama Wetlands / 232
Andrew Saunders
    A Classic Look at Ivan, the Storm / 234
Kate Seawell
    Brown Pelicans / 235
Glenda Richmond Slater
    Beach Cocoon / 237
R. T. Smith
    Jubilee / 238
Betty Spence
    Blackberry Picking 101 / 239
Catherine A. Swender
    Spanish Moss / 240
Seth Tanner
    Painted Turtle / 241
Peggy Teel
    Pink Pelican / 242
Margaret Vann
    Little River Lily / 243

VII. History Remembers

Helen Blackshear
    Muskogee Legacy / 247
Diann Blakely
    Little Boy Blue / 248
Robert Collins
    The Antichrist in Alabama / 249
Michael S. Harper
    American History / 251
Dorothy Diemer Hendry
    Mama's New Gown / 252
Jennifer Horne
    WPA / 253
Ruth Gunter Mitchell
    The Powers That Tried / 263
Minnie Bruce Pratt
    On the Road to Selma / 264
James Miller Robinson
    At Big Spring Park / 269
Christopher Singleton
    The Typewriter / 270

Notes and Acknowledgments / 271

Contributors / 275

Editors, *Whatever Remembers Us* / 304

I.

Places Remember

Bruce Alford

Rappelling at Eagle's Point

I stand at Eagle's Point,
the highest place in Alabama.
The trees look like Azalea plants.
The shadow of a cloud
moves over the valley.

In one tiger's leap
I no longer need
a preacher, as the rope
tricks through my hand
tightening, voiceless.

This is a lot like seeing
life flash before your eyes.
After a while, the trees
look like ballet lines,

girls standing at point.
Three miles deep,
a boy is being pushed down
the street on his first real bike.
Then I see myself standing

at the edge of a road
spitting across a ditch,
and I remember
this is how it all started:

cutting a vine
with a butcher knife
and swinging on it
for days until it broke.

Jerri Beck

Driving to Montgomery

"There's an unloved house," you say,
sweeping your arm to the right
where kudzu and sawbriars define
rotting walls and sagging roof.
"Houses collapse if no one loves them."
Like people, I think, picturing your mother
at the end of the drive. I twist to watch
the house out of sight. Kudzu flowers send
the odor of grape Kool-Aid after us.

How fragile the car seems—merely steel
between us and a world of asphalt
and unloved houses. The fields at home bloom
with abandoned cars and washing machines.
Great steel gardens border the road; morning
glories weave purple and pink through rusty hoods
and broken lids. One old, blue Ford has sat
so long alone that a jack pine stands in its trunk.

Driving to Montgomery on this clear Sunday,
I feel the car filling with the sadness
of unloved things: eyeless dolls in dusty
attic boxes, wheelless bikes leaning against
garage walls, dresses hidden in closets,
unread books, brown leaves raked to the curb,
letters stacked unopened on the desk.
Forty years of chipped dishes and worn-out shoes
fill basement corners. Six boxes of Mason jars,
long-empty, gather dust; the rings have rusted.
How easily we ignore used pieces of our lives.
Reluctant to let them go, we give them over
to hidden places where we do not have to see
the fading paint and rotting threads.

A stray dog, his skin clinging to sharp bones,
sniffs a bag of garbage beside the highway.
His eyes watch the car move past, but his nose
keeps its search. I start to cry—or the dog,
the house, the cars and all the things we
shut out, seal up, bury, move away from, and hide
so we won't have to love them any more.

Jack B. Bedell

My Son Discovers the Draw of Water
Samuel, Gulf Shores, 2005

He was still getting used to the sand between his toes
when the cool Gulf water crashed around his thighs,
knocking him back, then drawing him closer to home.
It took barely a second for his face
to go from complaint to laughter, for him to feel
the rhythm of the tide, to taste the salt
splashing his smile. Three steps forward, two steps
back. Again and again. All light and love.
It wasn't until the water reached his chest
he realized this was more than a game of chase,
more than simple joy, and that all pleasures
come with a price. He turned to shore and cried
for us to bring him back to the heavy sand.

T. J. Beitelman

The World Peace Poem
Birmingham, Alabama, May 2003

This is a day that seeks no documentation,
per se: a nothing day—later I will shampoo
the rug. There are men working on the A/C
in my apartment; it is warm. I have found
a café, an open table outside, and Highland
Avenue buzzes with a strange parade: Doo
Dah Day—people of various stripes bring
their dogs to the tidy little park down
the way. The dogs are leashed humanely—
harnesses of ingenious design. Hundreds
of smiling canine eyes, wagging tails, tongues.
Their people wear sunglasses. It's a zoo.
But a pleasant one. Tops are down. Friendly,
liberal, folksy music spills into the street.
All manner of preferences prevail. In
a place such as this, anything is possible:
a Big Blue Marble of peace, balanced budgets
everywhere, an appreciation for the world's
sundry beauties—physical, political, muscled
or not, a sprawling range of sticker prices.
There, a dachsund—taffy-stretched; here,
a Jack Russell. Yonder, a perfect mutt puppy.
Here comes a beautiful old woman in a pink dress.
There goes a Volvo, a stroller pushed happily
by a thin man and his plump wife. Now
reggae—Marley—*Don't worry about a thing.*
Sweet songs, melodies pure and true.
Rottweilers, a Ridgeback. Dobermans in
tricked out pick-ups. Handsome, bronzed
gay men. There are silly hats, Newfoundlands.
Yappy Pekinese. Bonnie Raitt. In such a
world as this, isn't it a perennial Saturday?
Isn't it just warm enough for the Sheepdogs

to open their mouths in a smiley half-pant?
Isn't there just enough breeze? Aren't there
wispy clouds enough, blue-sky enough, poems
enough, and pretty-people-to-marry enough?
Can this very day metastasize, spread out
concentrically from our Magic City's ground
zero? When will it reach Iceland? What on earth
will they do with all that warm breeze?

Margaret Key Biggs

The Rattling of Bones

People are always asking me
why I left Florida to come home
to Alabama. "Most people
do it the other way around," they say.
Feebly I answer that the highways are
too straight, and everything is always green,
Also, there are no seasons well-defined.
Most people passing through do not see
the esoteric beauty of my native Alabama;
they see only what interstates have to offer.
From Cheaha to Mobile Bay are
splendid scenes that beg the poet to write.
Yet, for all of the waterfalls, the rugged mountains,
the unbelievable colors of autumn or a shy spring,
it is even more that calls to me. Except for
my Revolutionary War ancestor and his wife,
all of my family's bones lie in red clay—
spread across this beloved place.
And thousands of cousins I have never met
live not too far from the Tallapoosa River;
it is strange how we have followed that river.
Stranger still is the rattling of bones I hear
when decisions are very important.
As old as I am, they drum out a code
that says, "Child, this way; don't go there."
I heed the messages those bones send,
and that is the real reason I am back here.
They said to me, "Come home. Come back to Alabama."

Jeff Blake

My Alabama Home

I see a thousand falling stars at night
falling, falling from the sky
on this my Alabama Home.
I see a steel mill belching smoke.
I hear a whippoorwill.
There goes a dove, a quail, a deer.
I see the Iron Man on the hill.
I smell a paper mill.
I see the cotton pickers and their bags.
The neighbors raise a barn.
I walk along the pristine bay.
I look for arrowheads in the fields
where Creek and Cherokees once roamed.
Helen Keller says "water," simply "water"
and her dark night is turned to day.
I hear a deep south, southern drawl.
A canopy of kudzu blankets every hill.
There's gospel music on the radio:
"Rock of Ages, cleft for me. Let me
hide myself in Thee."
My neighbor has a banjo on his knee.
The world's space frontier begins right here.
I see the antebellum homes, the magnolias
in their bloom, the dogwoods and azaleas
everywhere in spring.
The watermelons are to eat, "but not before the 4th."
There's okra, squash, corn, tomatoes and
so much more. There's pecan pie, sweet potato pie,
banana pudding; a table spread.
I hear the sound of a bomb, of screams, of dogs,
of fear. They ride the bus, they cross the bridge,
and shed their blood; martyrs for a noble cause.
I hear his thunderous voice from Dexter Avenue.
I love these rivers: the Alabama, the Coosa,

the Tombigbee, the Tennessee. I love the fall
when leaves turn gold and yellow and crimson red.
I miss the Bear and the gridiron duel.
I miss Bethel on a hill, the old cemetery out back.
I miss Thanksgiving at MaMa's house.
I miss playing dominos and rook.
I miss Grandmother on Christmas Day.
I hear Hank Williams' mournful song
about a poor old Indian who never got a kiss.
So many places on this earth I have roamed. So much
I have seen and learned. So many people have crossed
my path and taught me on the way. But, in the quiet
stillness of this hour, I still remember home.
My Alabama home.

Ray Bradbury

Poem Written On A Train
Just Leaving A Small Southern Town

Druid City, Druid City, what a pity what a shame,
Until noon of April 16th, I had never heard your name.

Is the all of you a forest, is the sum of you deep wood?
After midnight, then, what happens in your gnarled oak
        neighborhood?

Alabama is your mater, is your pater yonder oak?
Did you wander here from Memphis or from Celtic Roanoke?

That is if Roanoke was Celtic, and if not, then where and when
Did a shambling host of chestnuts plant you here in rainfall glen?

Just this side of Tuscaloosa, did the syrup: Pepper/Coke
Drown your acorns, spout your rootlings, high in mobs of elm
        and oak?

Do your priests survive in traffic, evil cops on every beat?
Do their acolytes teach sapling-innocents in every street?

Does your secret population rise at twilight, shunning sun?
Were they here before the pilgrims, centuries before Bull Run?

Druid City, Alabama, was your mama mystic fen?
Did the village smithy shape you with his devil's anvils--when?

In that anvil chorus forest, were the natives scrawny, few?
Was your natal floral fatal, rank persimmon, morbid yew?

Was the raping of the Sabines carried out in centaur deeps
Where, in central Alabama, Alexander, mad Pope, sleeps?

True or untrue, glad to see you, gladder still to see you gone;
Druid City, rainfalled, misting . . . sunk in locomotive dawn. [1]

Joanne Ramey Cage

Red Clay Poet

I can stand anywhere on Mount Cheaha,
drink in the crystal air like homemade wine,
stretch out my arms and feel this planet's pulse
like my own lifeblood reeling through my veins.
I close my eyes and search my soul for truth,
and find my love for earth is rooted deep
in mountain vales, and born of wind and rain.
I love this rock-strewn, corn- and cotton-sown
sweet Alabama land, and all the earth
spread out around it; sand and sea I love,
as far as clock or chain can rule or mark.
Here on a rock I stand in Alabama,
my thoughts like wings unfurled against the sky,
and hug the whole rough world against my heart.

Mark Dawson

Lunch with Kelley at the Montgomery Museum of Fine Arts Café M

My coat draped across the extra chair
Was like a third person. You didn't care
About my awkwardness, or that I stole
A glance at your reflection in the window.
I hoped your legs would brush against mine
Beneath our tiny, wooden table.
                              When
We stood outside to part, it seemed a second
Sign—your blush, I mean. The first, I reckoned,
Was the way your hair settled softly
Against your neck, while, matter-of-factly,
A pair of geese flew across the lake,
Just above the water and leaving no wake.

Tom Drinkard

The Post Office

WAS the Federal Government
in Falkville, Alabama.
The flag flew year-round:
Official.
I couldn't see over the counter,
and walked quietly... almost on tiptoe.
The unsmiling gray postmistress
(who always knew who was sending what
to whom)
watched suspiciously.
NO SPITTING ON THE FLOOR, and
NO LOITERING; the signs warned potential spitters and loiterers.
One wall held a moldering jumble of **ARMED AND DANGEROUS!**
pictures of ordinary-looking, unhappy people
hung from a curved wire hook;
almost too high for me to read their crimes.

Two hundred boxes glittered
with square, curlicued brass doors
holding glass windows to see exciting things inside;
a knurled knob in the center surrounded by numbers
and a butterfly-shaped latch key
that turned to open the box,
if your memory was right.

Birthday cards, notes from special aunts,
and sometimes, wonderful grimy pink cards saying,
PARCEL TOO LARGE FOR BOX,
made me stand tall daily to peer
through finger-smeared glass.
A faded map of the United States,
splitting at the edges from heat and age,
decorated the wall opposite the boxes;
our home town was there:

The center of five concentric circles;
a small red dot,
like the pivot point of a drawing compass;
the rest of the world was widening rings.

II

The shrinking town,
bypassed by the new Interstate highway,
became somewhere to go on long holiday weekends,
or in summer;
like dating a local girl
encountered at a high school class reunion;
(remembered, fondly, as pretty; but,
grown somehow plain, and. . .
dressed out of fashion)
when there was nothing else to do.

Summer-separation notes,
some perfumed, some witty missives;
were almost-daily delight,
I ripped them open and read them twice
hungry for repetitive sweetness,
or radical old ideas,
so university-new.

On the wall map above,
black circles surrounded the red dot,
constricting like steel bands.
Blinking my way outside, hand outstretched,
on the blinding hot sidewalk
the air felt thick, hard to breathe;
autumn was far away.

III

P.O. Box 217, etc.,
the computers recorded with my name and numbers,
as the **Home of Record** demanded by the Army.

A permanent home address
for mail.

Occasional written reports,
dispatched to that box,
had paratrooper wings or berets
decorating the envelopes,
from Forts Benning, Monmouth or Bragg,
until,

the postmark became **APO 96222**.
the dateline inside (always),
Saigon: (for Mother's peace of mind).

The black U.S. Government ballpoint pen
spelled out home's name and numbers
quickly, automatically,
as a compass needle spins
and seeks magnetic North.

Bored mail clerks
handed damp envelopes from a canvas bag
to the lucky ones.

A smeared gray-black circle on or near the stamp;
the P.O. name and date
from that small red dot,
like the pole star
shimmered as a constant.

IV

After jet-lag sleep,
I walked, on wooden-block feet,
the short hike
(that once had been a major expedition)
to Main Street.
The town sat in the July Alabama sun,
like a shrunken, tired old man
who has nothing else to do. . .

jarring; like the first sight of a beloved relative
visited after years of separation,
who has unaccountably aged.

The railroad siding rusted silently in ragged weeds:
trains no longer stopped. . .
the old Post Office building;
not gone, but part of a general store.

Almost-familiar faces
swam up out of the wavy afternoon heat
saying my name.
Casually speaking, nodding,
passing by as if we had been in church together
the afternoon before.

The new Post Office:
close to the old site,
hardly larger, but air conditioned, with green tile floors,
and smooth brushed-steel doors with stamped black numbers
on each box,
only a small keyhole in the bottom center. . .
efficient. Probably safer.
While using the brass key
that said, **DO NOT DUPLICATE**,
and dragging out a jam of four-color sale notices;
a man whose yard I had mowed as a teenager,
noticed me;
"Already back from Vietnam?
seems like you just left.
How long were you there?"
His wattled neck thrust down and out of the khaki shirt,
stretched and corded like a terrapin's;
faded blue eyes holding me:
"More than a year,"
not counting, for him,
the hours.
"My, my,
It don't seem like that long.
You wasn't wounded, was you?"
(peering more curiously)

"No holes in my skin," he was satisfied.
"Where do you live now?"
". . . Don't know yet,"
". . . well. . ."

Turning away,
waving a vague good-bye over his shoulder,
not looking back,
he pushed out into the street,
high-top work shoes scuffling;
bottoms of his striped overalls dragging.

Alone, and the air too cold
for one just back from the tropics;
waiting to meet someone else
seemed a waste of time.

I left there to find home. [2]

Deborah Ferguson

While Driving Through Alabama's Black Belt

Planted along paved roads
lined with magnolia and sycamore,
in towns scarcely known, called
Eutaw, Uniontown and Greensboro
are elderly Black men,
once called Colored and Negro.
Lifeless eyes reflect forgotten terror.
Distress,
    desire,
        disappointment
[have] cultivated the stalks
of their bodies, each face
evolved into a soul harvest.
 Dried,
   discarded,
      discontinued
corn husks, cotton bolls, banana peels
and apple cores, planted in pristine overalls
waiting, waiting for Death's recycling.

John Finlay

The Road to the Gulf

A small white town, its silver water-tank
Gleaming above a green deep river's bank,
We passed before the pastures still unmowed
And melons piled for sale beside the road.
Samples were cut on shells of oyster blue,
So ripe the seedless heart had split in two.
The closer to the Gulf we came the more
The flattened earth recalled itself as shore.
The needle of the pine, metallic leaf,
Grew where lusher life would come to grief.
The soil lay dreaming of the ancient salt,
A trance of heat inside the summer's vault.
It cooled by evening when we reached the bay.
Black vistas opened out; just miles away,
We felt the plunging shelves of rising sea.
The boats were in; at shore beneath a tree
The scaling boys half-naked, brown as nuts,
Threw to the blue crabs the fishes' guts. [3]

Abby Frierson

Alabama Vistas

I stand in downtown Mobile,
watch Mardi Gras floats roll past.
Years of riding the floats or watching
is never enough, never grows old.
We store doubloons and tri-colored necklaces,
symbols of transient happiness.
They gather dust in our closets.

I stand on sugar-pale beaches,
watch the sun sink into the Gulf,
and paint the sand scarlet gold.
A ghost crab scuttles past my feet,
a gull finds his supper.
A ray leaps out of the surf.
Dolphins gossip in the waves.
Sandcastles dot the shoreline, their makers long gone.
Crabs investigate and burrow underneath.

I stand on a mountain,
look down on a sea of trees.
Loblollies rise above the others,
stretching over them like mothers
watching their toddlers.
A mountain stream bathes my feet,
ricochets off boulders in its stony bed.
The call of a yellowhammer echoes
through the loblollies.

Maurice Gandy

Church Street Cemetery: Mobile, Alabama

Around infant tombs of brick and mortar
few hopeless inches raised
above the reaching grass,
monument and urn thud down unheard
in the sodded sand.
Slabs with intricate concern for the soul
have been granulated by wind and rain—
records of great pain made glyphs,
faded as any childhood myth
to be puzzled over by the vine
in its long, groping climb
after light.

Is this how the children end?
Buried by rubble
of dreams fallen in?
They lost the road
and they can't go back
and no one will ever know.
Now no one will ever know.

Dear Lord Of Us
On Some Morning Glorious
Cleave This Brick And Stone
Embrace These Tiny Bones
And Gently Bear Them
Gently Home.

Virginia Gilbert

The Casting of Lots
Auction, Downtown Huntsville, 2002

Once there was money and the newest gadgets—
the pulley gears and wheels above the rusted vent
for the attic fan, but now the whole second floor ceiling
is water stained and rotted, spilling guts and bits
of dust and fragments from the century before
on the disfigured cardboard boxes stuffed

with dead life. I did not know you, the owner
of this house, but strangers like me today walk
over your mahogany floors, looking at
what you left behind. In the basement
is a black, horsehair reclining couch layered
in coal dust; a primitive x-ray machine presses

against the opposing wall. Every hat
your doctor husband had worn must be here,
the brims caked with sweat lines, and your
straw hats, too, big, floppy with flowers
and holes, are up for sale. A nephew
conducts this business, tells us you

are not dead, but in a home now,
too old and frail to live in your house,
too old and frail to tend your possessions.
So what is left of you? Even your privacy
is gone. White shutters are half closed over
blackened windows. A cement urn
by the front porch steps is shattered
and the other is missing. In a few days, all
your history will be sold. I see the mockingbird
skiff quickly around the porch's rim; in spring,
the wasp nest by the gingerbread brace
will buzz. With repair, the dark oak doors

will open again to friends. Eventually,
a gardener will cut back the tangled chokeberries
by the drawing room's emptied window. It's leading,
I swear, looks like outspread hands pressed
desperately against the glass—"Let me in!
Let me in! Oh, God, let me back in—"

Andrew Glaze

Red Mountain
Birmingham, 1973

Tu Fu said
" I climbed West on Incense Burner Mountain—
I will erase the dust from my face
and live in the place I love
separated forever from the world of men."

Sometimes I almost guess where that may be,
when the low sheepflock clouds pass running
into the northeast and are caught
tumbling against the pinetops of the hills—
and above, the sunfish of the second layer high

are flattened and swim portly across to the South—
while the starlings like smoke
boil up out of the ruined sycamores
and turbulent loblolly.
The mammoth Silurian hummocks of the storm front
coast in brushing away the barely commencing stars.

It isn't here below that I thrive and belong,
on this mechanized macerated staring sod,
but up in that turbulent
liquid element where everything is changing,
being blown from Mountain Rock to Endless Plain River,
to the past changing of the sun and moon.

John Halbrooks

Exeter Book Riddle 8: A Gulf-Coast Paraphrase

Ic thurh muth sprece   mongum reordum . . .

I speak through a mouth   with many tongues,
and sing of tricks,   change my voice
with sass.

hlude cirme . . .

    I cry out loudly.
You can't stop me, sugar,   from speakin' my mind,
old evening-singer.   To folks I bring
joy on the bayou,   when I call out
my many voices,
    as they recline
on their porches.

Saga hwæt ic hatte . . .

    Say what I'm called,
I who mimic   all sorts of foolishness,
dive-bomb your cat,
and shout for all to hear,   and cheer y'all with
my many voices,
    the best old songs.

Andrew Hudgins

Ashes

Bill gripped the can in both hands and sashed it upward,
casting into the March air his cousin, a man
I'd met a time or two, but now a cloud
of ash and bone grit launched above the river,
and the wind, which bloweth where it listeth, this time
amused itself to swirl the ashes overhead
and, at the moment I yawned, it slapped them back
across the clustered mourners. I sucked down
a grainy mouthful of fresh death, coughed, gagged,
and everyone surged toward me, hands outstretched.
They swatted at my dusty hair, brushed death's
gray epaulets off my shoulders and thumped my back
furiously, as if this dust were different
from other dust, and it was—or why would I
have dressed in coat and tie, and stood, head bowed,
on the soft bank of the Black Warrior, watching
huge barge trains humped with coal chug to the Gulf
while some young Baptist mumbled pieties?
I hacked death from my lungs and spat death out
and hacked up more. The mourners drummed the loose
death out of me. "I'm okay. Thanks," I said,
but they kept drumming, drumming on my back.
"Leave me alone!" I snapped, and we all glanced,
ashamed, into each other's ash-dappled faces.
We turned back to the river and its commerce,
the sermon and its commerce, the wind's new commerce,
and breathed it in and breathed it out and breathed it in. [4]

J. P. Jones

Remembering Alabama from Japan

Alabama, the most beautiful word I know.
You're the home of my family, my friends,
a place of complete relaxation after a day's work,
a view of the past intertwined with the present.

Alabama, a song in my heart forever.
You're memories of my childhood—both good and bad.
I'll never trade you, my number one home of all-time,
A classy portrait carefully framed with rich history.

Alabama, a beauty that causes envy from all.
You're a quiet summer evening with sweet tea
      and a porch swing,
Home to fragrant pines and life lived slow and steady.
You are unmatched throughout the union—
      you true Southern Belle.

Alabama, tall mountains, cozy beaches in the moonlight,
and canyons that invoke reverence from all.
I hear your sweet voice beckoning me to return to my roots.
Patiently waiting, you prepare a special place just for me.

Alabama, I will return to you one day.
My solemn promise shall not be broken, I swear.
High on one of your mountains, I'll come again.
For eternity, I'll rest beneath your great sky.

Willie James King

Old Cahawba

South, west of Selma
off Highway-22,
on a slab of stone
the name is carved:
Old Cahawba, The First
Capital of Alabama,
and fifty-yards,
maybe more,
at the confluence
of the Alabama river
and the Cahawba river
is a solid plank of iron,
an auction block,
not worn by water,
undefiled by lichen
and time. I
am certain: It
was built
to last,
forever.

Thomas Lakeman

Driving On Through Foley, Alabama

The wheels of human enterprise are swift:
Less than a hundred years ago, this road
On which we drive was not a town at all,
But only grass and advertising for
A place still mainly yet to be decided on.
A planned community envisioned on a plain
Of undifferentiated pine
And hard-packed clay too stubborn for much planting
And so available at a steal. Stolen,
One could say, but dearly bought by those
Who left behind their other dreams of home
And gave themselves whole-hearted to the work
Of making from this placid ground a place:
And yes, well-named and well-conceived
Along straight late Victorian lines, promising
Intersections of gardening and commerce,
Meant to grow in stately arcs and sweeps,
Just as children here were meant to grow
By sturdy steps from babies into town folk,
Not too fancy for their roots, nor too wild
To disregard the good of staying put.

And yet the place would never be constrained:
I found it so. And as I drive along
The road that joins the old town to the new
I see how awkwardly and out of plumb
The town's two halves were joined. There is
No evolution from the oak-lined streets
To giant metal buildings hawking God.
The town is not a lady come to tea; it is
A boisterous sullen teen with breaking voice.

It jumps and squawks excitedly to life
Like a chicken crossing an eight-lane road,
Which is about how wide that road will be
Some day. I'm sure of it. Just as I know
One day it will be more than Spanish moss
Or even Wal-Mart and the outlet mall.
Though I would never dream of trying to guess
In what unplanned directions Foley wants
To grow. I still think nonetheless
It's going to make its streets run true
In time, and take its own sweet time
Deciding what to be when it grows up.

Irene Latham

The Quilts of Gee's Bend
after viewing the exhibit at the Whitney Museum, March 2003

They hung like Jesus on bare walls,
far from the curve in the Alabama River
where they were born. Crowds gathered
and gawked as the quilts looked on,
silently accepting their fate
while the lives of their makers
were examined stitch by stitch.

There is no death for some things,
no story so simple that it can be told
without color or form. See
the edges where wildflowers grow?
The sides lined with bands of corduroy
marching against the grain?
The bars of crimson rising like *Hallelujah!*
in a church on Sunday morning?

The spirit emerges with or without
resurrection and lives in the denim
strips salvaged from worn work pants.
If you listen, you can hear them whispering
their prayers for the children
they have held and helped conceive,
the sick they have nursed
and the dead they could not save,
for nights spent chasing dreams,
days spent snapping in a breeze.

Celia Vickery Lewis

Canoe, Alabama, 1961

The summer we pulled up cockleburs
For a penny apiece
I was only six
And knew nothing.

Our uncle's plan was to appease our aunt
Who knew our days of leisure to be numbered
Though for us they rolled towards heaven
As endlessly as Abraham's heirs.

We thought life was one wide indigo river
To disembark from and get back onto
At anytime. But Lord, now we know
That life is one hard row to hoe.

Carey Link

My Alabama Home

I left a monotonous
cacophony of honked horns, ringing phones,
suburban town homes with sound proof barriers for backyards,
55 mph speed limits,
smoke rising from fuel plants to turn air brown

for the seeds of furrowed fields
that grow beneath open sky.
Long trips down back roads.
To climb into the hollow
of a high tree.
To feel warm breeze on my cheeks.
To sit at Sunday suppers of fried chicken,
potatoes, collard greens, black-eyed peas,
peach pie, and sweet tea.
To dry clothes on a line.
To find and keep treasures
cool, dark, deep.
To watch a yellow and black spider
weave the initials of her last breath—
a geometric code of where she has been
and will go
on my window.
To listen to stories of the past and present
whispered on a porch swing
as sun melts behind clouds
in the shadow of evergreen.

Susan Luther

Two Views of Howard's Chapel

*a memorial to Sally Howard
constructed by Col. Milford W. Howard
at the North entrance of De Soto State Park, Ft. Payne,
1930's*

I.

There is this huge
knuckle of God—at least
somebody thought so—em-
braced by a chapel. Somebody

sited the building right around
one of the biggest rocks you've ever seen.
It's huge: way higher than a woman's
head: and outside, the cross-topped jagged block looks
like some—I don't know what—some stone-
skinned hybrid out of "Star Trek"—devouring
civilization like a cinema sarsen.

Really, who'd conceive a ridiculous thing like that?
At least it attracts the tourists—
and campers, I suppose,
on Sunday morning, all sweaty
from hiking the river path
to get there, in muddy jogging shoes
and dusty jeans. Their jaws must drop wide

open when they see the whole back wall and altar's
　　the behind of Old Granddaddy Rock
(They must think: "It takes an Alabama redneck!")—
There's some verse or other on it
out of the Bible, or something. Seriously,
you ought to see it—we'll run up

next time you visit—
those little yellow flowers by the doorstep—I've never
been sure of their name—ought to be out
about April. And the churchyard—it's so quiet there—
blooms halfway to heaven, this time of year.

II.

Immortality

God Has All Ways Been As Good To Me As I Would Let Him Be

When the rough pines burr
their wind songs
God's just clearing His throat

& if His funnel bell should sweep
the mountains clean
eventually   He will make them new

new trees, new mountains   All things
the Lord hath made
& unmade He shall remake

Take me into your heart oh God
the stony fist
schist chrysalis

and cupped hand budding
to silk-brush   & a burst
of seed   Lord

conceive me   bear me
as the child

who would be found

Lord, I pray make me happy.
But God don't let me forget how I cried. [5]

James Mersmann

**Chilton County Woods:
Revisiting the Garden in Ruins**

The fences have fallen,
the pine posts cut and skinned
in Alabama heat, rotted through in three years,
the wire still gleaming like new in the weeds.

I knew then they would not hold,
but the work was the need,
the perfect perfection of the line
of wire stretching into the trees
and the sweat rolling and purging the city
crud and a thousand years of bad marriage.

Alone I dug the holes, alone
sighted them in, and the poles
cut at a slant to shed the rain
stood straight, and my goats watched

as if wondering what it was I wanted
to wall away from them in this lost
nowhere of wilderness.

It was nothing but what is alive
because of human touch, whether radishes
or beans or truth, or something so simple
as your eyes watching now without lies

or something so old
as the arrowheads that sprouted in the lettuce rows
after rains, broken triangles of rose
quartz finely shaped and serrated
by a hand before Christ in a dream of animal thighs

or that single, tapered stone,
lifted by the thrusting asparagus,
chipped from chert and dropped by Clovis man, pointed
and waiting for me twelve thousand years,
that I, finding it, might at last
harvest one thing hard and whole. [6]

William Miller

The Moon in Delta, Alabama

It rises through the trees,
floods the backyards
and low fields,
reflects from every tin roof
in the valley.

The white stones
of the graveyard are lit,
the beds of trucks
parked on dirt roads.

And the lake holds more
than its share—
light searching
even the bottom weeds.

Everyone stops, looks up
from gray windows,
blankets spread
in the open air,
a boat drifting out
from the shore.

*Tomorrow, things will
be different, the air
this clear, the sky
brighter than noon . . .*

Slowly, the mountain
takes it back.

Light retreats from
pine needles, goes out
of the tall grass
like dew.

Cheaha swallows
the great stone whole,
just as the Indians said.

And the night
is hidden, once more,
safely from the day.

Mary Murphy

Mostly Home

Mobile—
the home I intended to leave,
but could never coordinate
desire
with time, money, or
a yard sale or U-haul.

Instead, even when traveling,
I wanted to return home
to the place pulled together and apart
by hurricanes, politics, or the paving of roads,
where recipes for gumbo, fish batter, and fried chicken
are heritage as much as name.

Tree limbs scrape the top of cars.
Possums and raccoons waddle across yards
to raid trash cans undisturbed by barking dogs,
hissing cats, or passing cars.

Dew Drop, Cannon, Old Shell, and Spring Hill,
all have meanings and jokes
few outsiders understand.

Mardi Gras, where people can hide in public
is condemned by many
and attended by most.

Thunderstorms move across the bay,
chase white caps and dump
twenty-minute floods on the city.
Still on a Sunday morning
at Barnes and Noble, with coffee
and *The New York Times*, horrors of the world
or secluded vacation spots in the Pacific,
you can look up from your table

to see people greet each other—
dressed for fishing or church
and oblivious to the social trinity
of the haunted Southern city. [7]

Susan Murphy

Who D`Ya Pull For?

I'm a transplant, glad to be.
Alabama's home to me.
I came from ice and snow and waste
To blossom in this temperate place.

The transfer wasn't really hard,
Driver's license, voter's card,
With thirty days to rearrange
License plates and address change.

The only thing with urgency?
My choice in the state's rivalry.
Blue and orange? Red and white?
Will you yell "War Eagle" or "Roll Tide"?

You can't be neutral; you must pick
Or else be labeled heretic.
The lines are drawn. All doubt is treason
Especially during football season.

Weddings, christenings, burials
Are planned around these schedules.
Moms-to-be know they must slow
Their labor pains 'til the halftime show.

And then in the November cold,
Both teams meet in Iron Bowl
Where flags are flown, fight songs sung
As fans fill up the stadium,

Or ticketless, hunch knee-to-knee
Around some big wide screen TV
To cheer and boo and hiss and gasp
For bragging rights within their grasp.

Hours later, energy spent,
Winners gloat, losers lament
And vow that next year they will see
A glorious vengeful victory.

This does not mean they will not stop
To change your tire in the parking lot.
It's just tradition, a lifelong strain
'Tween Tuscaloosa and The Plains.

Yes, Alabama welcomed me
With gracious hospitality.
It will welcome you, just plan ahead.
Auburn blue or Bama red?

Helen Norris

Capitol City Yesteryear

You know those buildings wedge-shaped
In the older part of town.
A city street will stop bewildered
And then split along the arrow head
With twin streets fanning out, forgetting
Like children leaving home.

You know those buildings like an ax-blade
Slicing the city's heart in two
The way a woman's heart is cut
Two ways between one lover and another
Between a lover and a child
Between a life of sun and son
And one with furious wakings
Into days that spin in darkness
Threads to weave another dark.

You know those women who will stop
Bewildered like a city street
And break in two.

Phyllis Peck

Musings from a Small Alabama Town

Not far from the noise
Of a crowded highway,
On the bluffs of Mobile Bay,
I live a quiet life.

Founders taught me
To love the arts,
To welcome all who came,
To attune to nature,
To love all its manifestations.

I hear them still . . .
But change comes,
Invading with ways
Often unlike our own.

We see the blight of growth
And so we plan,
And plan again,
Trying to have it all—
Old traditions,
New neighbors.

Georgette Perry

Montgomery, 1922

Mother, I still hear your stories
when I listen to the fire sermon of the past
that lets lips move in brown photos in the album,
or when I hold the tattered Bible,
its cover crumbling in my hands like ashes.
George Stuart Wilson's name is written there
in the strong hand of Martha his wife,
and the day of his death, October second.

In Montgomery an old crime
drops like a stone to a pond.
There's someone's rage, quick as a cottonmouth.
I don't know whose, or who lies dead from it.
I'm blind as the two policemen, one my grandfather,
through dusty streets searching for the killer.
They find only a braggart in a tavern.
My grandfather wrestles to disarm him.
His partner's panicky shot goes wild.
The man George Wilson, shot through the eye,
falls away from, is not even the murderer.

If a prayer could save you
past and future would ripple and blur,
but from my heart I speak a fool's prayer:

> *Don't die, good man, grandfather I never saw.*
> *Live wise as Odin and never grieve your loss.*

Two days you linger.
When Martha bends by your bed you know her.
At home Sadie, twelve, tends little Elizabeth.

Don't die and leave the moment,
the sun through the hospital window
hanging in glare an hour from the horizon
never to ease in rose forgiveness down.

There's left a tiny pension, Spanish American War,
and a house on a wide street with willow oaks.
For years the paint will grey and peel,
boards on the porch splintering underfoot,
pipes rusting and leaking upstairs,
the rooms there full of chancy renters.
If her father were alive, Sadie wouldn't leave so young
to teach in the two-room country school.
I see her dark eyes and olive skin.
She's bobbed and crimped her indian hair.
A beau from high school follows to court her there.
My gaze is quiet as the grass
under the restless shadows of mother and father.

To pray for the past is to gainsay God
all the way back, deciding how the world will be.
If a prayer could save you, Grandfather,
some other lanky child would take my place,
spending the summers under your roof,
naming the oaks and telling them stories.

October second, 1922. The light sets out from Mizar
that tonight, if I look north, will prick my eyes.
In ragged grass near the Montgomery house
a strand of goldenrod holds a butterfly.
Its soft wings barely brushing clash like cymbals,
the nowhere future collapsing to now.

Marge Piercy

Becoming mobile in Mobile

I attended an academic conference in Mobile
in full hot sultry spring in a relapsed hotel.
For two days I listened. A ghetto teacher told us
my poems worked there. A professor used Derrida
to weave a shimmering fantasy web of critique.
An angry nun from Minnesota hated GONE TO
SOLDIERS because those nasty Jews picked
up rifles instead of practicing passive
resistance, staying morally pure like her.

By third day, my ears were stuffed with awkward
words; I had become a feather pillow. Mary
Murphy, grad student who worked in E.R.,
rescued me. We ran off together in her car,
out on the causeway to Fairhope for shrimp
fresh out of the bay and cold beer. It was
a day blue as campanula, the air soft
and salty, the water shimmering, lapping
as if no storm could ever ruffle it.

She spoke of emergency room nights.
"I never knew a person could set fire
to someone they love." She rescues
dogs; I rescue cats. We watched shrimp
boats on the horizon. Ten years later
we reconnected at once. There are women
lean as poplars, strong as white oaks—
sound women who ring like tuning forks
true and clear when you try them.

Thomas Rabbitt

After the Flood

Love was not the Charles which, when I was young,
I tried to walk across. I jumped and swam
And my one friend yelled, *I won't rescue you!*
Counterpoint, I thought then. Point, I see now.
I swam back and emerged, covered with mud,
And we went for coffee in Harvard Square.
No one else knew I had done this mad thing
And would do it again in Alabama
The morning after another cold river
Retreated from the Promised Land to leave
Behind such a baptism of surprises:
The riverbank awash in shiny mud
And dying fish which, turning into fossils,
Could look both down on me and up to God.
     *

Once I knew a woman who called the park
On River Road the place where failed men walk.
Never the one to turn a phrase or trick—
A ponderous wit—she thought herself really
Too crushing as, indeed, she would have been
Had she, after her last jump, lit upon
Any of the life forms she loved to scorn.
Who could resist? Her splat was so much talk.
Isn't failure whatever spot you're in?
Here, along the riverwalk, after dark
Each failure is its own reward, or nearly,
When one's success is measured by the mouthful
And love lights up like little neon fishes,
God's flashy critics poisoning the blood. [8]

Tut Riddick

Spirit Square: York, Alabama

I lay on my bed and dreamed of owning a home,
a dog, and being me.
It happened.
I lay on my bed and dreamed of a place
where everybody counts.
It's happening.
I dreamed of a place where people are curious
to learn, understand each other, and accept differences.
It happened.
I've lain on my bed and dreamed of a place
with no jealousy, only encouragement and compassion,
where people shared and understood your poetry,
your longings, your heart.
It is beginning to happen.
I've dreamed of people traveling many paths to truth,
not crowding each other on theirs.
They laugh, love, and move on.
It's going to happen.
There'll be a place of no uniforms,
at home in caftans, sombreros, blue jeans,
Walking sticks, diapers, beach pajamas.
Wow! What a show!
What a conflagration of the mind!
I dream of a place where people garden,
bake bread, cook soup,
make quilts, knit afghans, construct books,
read about Botswana,
and talk about everything.
In rockers on the sidewalk or
benches made by hand . . .
We're getting there
and we're calling it Spirit Square.

Sue Scalf

Montgomery, 1990

Here by the river in the mist
of mock orange, Spanish moss and magnolia,
Southern clichés of humid days, warm rains,

the city sits,
dowager and debutante.
Here is the dignity of old homes and giant trees

and, at the fringes, golf courses in gentle swells,
a splash of interstate.
Downtown, Bell Street with its red brick

of public housing, mule-earred chairs on porches,
leads to Union Station. Dexter
slopes to the capitol's bronze star,

the Confederate flag still flying,
the fountain spraying mist and rainbows.
On Madison, red-necked farmers unload produce,

listen to their wives who bake, crochet,
grow gourds and collards.
Maids, returned from Chicago,

ride buses to Allendale, Thomas.
In winter bone-chilling rains swell the Alabama.
In summer, heat is a lotion

oily on the skin and burning.
Air-conditioners hum; sprinkler swirl
at the country club.

Here Scott and Zelda fluttered like tired moths
home to Mama Sayre and Felder.
Here King preached and Rosa Parks refused to move.

Montgomery sits as self-assured
as a grand dame at the D.A.R.,
Fanning, sipping mint tea.

Eric Smith

Cotton's Pond, 1982

When I surfaced,
nose breaching brown water
like a sword-tip,
like something come to life,
I sucked the leather palm of the preacher,
but he did not let me go,
a thick thumb and forefinger deftly delaying my rebirth.
His other hand stood me upright in the mud,
my toes sinking through
to the rotten, vegetable bottom.

I opened my eyes, chin-deep in bilge,
and the preacher let me breathe sunlight
sluiced through a fault in the soapy clouds
until I could stand again on my own.

On the bank, waiting
alone near the hoof-pitted edge of the world,
was my mother, weeping ash-black tears
that branched and traced the corners of her mouth
like an old marionette's.
And I gave her a son's sloppy embrace
before I had slogged fully ashore,
my eight years of sin buried behind
in the gray, fish-eaten silt of Cotton's Pond.

Marilyn Tarvin

Cotton and Calculus

Over the years, I've gauged growth in Huntsville
by where its cotton patches grew:
a small one on the square downtown,
or a large patch in Research Park.

It pleased me to think of rocket scientists
thinking deep calculus thoughts next to
cotton plants just thinking it's a good day to grow.
How can you take yourself too seriously
when you're rubbing elbows with a cash crop?

Huntsville's juxtaposition of technical and agrarian is gone,
but this rocket scientist remembers.

Donna Jean Tennis

Home from the Hunt:
Exploring River Run Gulf Course, Montgomery, AL

So long, you call, *I'm off*
to River Run to hunt for balls.

A harmless sport, to search among the grass
along the lake for dimpled spheres, thwacked
by sticks in hands that worship at the feet
of names like Palmer, Player, Nicklaus and the like.

A chance for me to sneak
some time alone.
Then, one day, at eventide, you ask,
How would you like to go along to hunt for balls?

We rattle in our cart down gravel paths, watching
balls tee off, to sail above the fairway,
    straight
        or doglegged,
            evading water hazards
        sandy traps,
    to the green,
where a cup is planted to receive the putt
(which may take *several* muttered thwacks).

Look, honey, a bunny sitting, oh, so still.
Not afraid of purring carts or swinging silver sticks.

Can't look now. I've found another ball.
Rabbits living near the fourteenth tee
produce a thriving family every year.

Near fairway five, the woods abound with teeming
life, wild berry vines, topaz-yellow peppers
used by Creeks and other tribes, thorny shrubs—
prehistoric trees trail twilight moss from twisted limbs.
Wait a bit, it's awfully dark in here.
What about snakes?

You wave a ball retriever in my face.
The man I love *hates* snakes! This man's
legs rise slim and tanned in rubber
hunting boots. Woven straw shades
an unaccustomed grin.

Fashion statement with an attitude.

Around the gloomy glade, concrete slabs dot
furrowed ground, tossed about like cellar doors
in Dorothy's tornado.
Brushing brambles aside, I read,
>Robert Bonaparte, died April 28, 1951
>Martha Gibb, September 9, 1928
>James Gibb, October 13, 1947

Other markers sleep enshrined in green.
No flowers bloom in this lost paradise.

The dirt beneath the slab of Robert B
has washed away. If we shine a torch
inside the breach, will we find scores
of small white balls at rest inside?

You apologize, your voice friendly
and familiar. *Excuse me, Mr. Bonaparte,
I have to cross your path to reach
that ball. How are you today, sir?*

Mosquitos bite the sunset air that reeks
of months of mower clippings left to molder
in the heat. Climbing back into our cart,
we drive into the summer light with one last
look at crumbling stones, while tangled woods
continue to reclaim their own.

Around another lake, the largest on the course,
where cottonmouth and moccasin glide in tolerant
togetherness, you wade along the bank, exploring
in the silt and slime like zealous Indy
searching for the Ark.

*Deep inside the woods one day, I came upon
two deer with fawn,* you say. *A rare and lovely
sight. Mallards nest here, too. Nine ducklings*

left the nest this spring. You swat a dragonfly.

You point out bamboo stands and tell of footpaths
through the woods where balls can lie in wait
from summer's thickest green to winter's clearest point.
We'll come back then, you claim, *to enjoy the hunt
without the fear,*—as though you've never felt
a moment's fear yourself.

The Cypress swamp, unchanged since time began,
crouches, thick and algae-laden in the dusk,
lodging alligator gar with needle-teeth
among decomposing stumps and ancient trees.

*It begins behind the cemetery, running past
thirteen, to the fourteenth tee. I've never seen
a full-grown gator while tramping in and out.*

The Tallapoosa River flows behind the course,
pumped into the many lakes, and then pumped
out again, to irrigate the greens.

Along the river, an Indian mound rises
above twelve acres of deeded land. Their land.
The Kolomi Creek, smooth-skinned braves
with hair of night and aged men of wisdom
weeping still for those they left behind who walked
the Trail of Tears. We drive in silence
past the densely wooded site.

Then, *This is great*, you cry. *I think I see
the mound. I'm going in. Wait here.*

At last, you reappear, snapping twigs
beneath your boots, crushing thickets
undisturbed for years.

Look, I found another one.
The next time you call, *so long, I'm off
to hunt for balls,* I'll sit beside the door,
like wives in earlier, less civilized times,
who waited and prayed for their men
to come home from the wars. [9]

Jeanie Thompson

At Moundville

At Moundville they called the river *long man*
    with its head in the mountains
        and its tail in the gulf
they saw how the world moved before them
    they touched the world with their eyes
        licked the earth from a baby's feet
today the Black Warrior snakes from my left
    to my right like a giant rope of sinuous touch
the wind's tiniest thermals laying upon it a transfer
    of crosshatching that burns deep
        what is the afterimage of touch
a red tail hawk flushes from the steep bank
    where I stand held back
        by a manmade boundary of rock and wire
the hawk dives into the thermals above the river
    floats with wings spread wide
        soars over the hardwoods
    the hawk cries *eeee* and *eeee* and *eeee*
lights once and flies again from sight
    below me the answering call of its mate
        and from across the river
the first hawk's call rises
    and fills me *eeee, eeee*
in the natural acoustics from bank to bank
    like my love cry to you
        it resonates beyond will or thought
what is the after image for touch
    the artisan took up a bone needle
        sketched crosshatches of the undisturbed river

with wind caressing it
      placed the object she had made
            in the reducing fire to make the pliable clay
strong, strong to hold water
      to cleanse their birthed child when she glistened
            blood-red in the fire light
to hold water that releases all after image of touch
      moving south
           carrying only its will
                its course upon its back
like the after image of touch
      that memory and release of love [10]

Doris Gabel Welch

My South

My South is
Hot
Humid
Sultry
Just like its women.

My South is
Crystal clear
Beads of condensation
Sliding down a tall glass
Of sweet iced tea
Adorned by a sprig of mint
And a slice of lemon.
It is slowly sipped
On a front porch
Framed by Jackson Vine
While one gently
Rocks or swings.

My South is
Antebellum mansions
Sharecropper shacks
With rusty tin roofs
Which match
The red clay earth
That nourishes
Stalks of white cotton
Mirroring the clouds above.

My South is
Sagging gray weathered barns
With faded painted roofs
That whisper
Morton Salt or
See Rock City.

My South is
Gentle words
Darlin'
Honey
Yes, Sir and No, M'am
And Y'all come back, y'hr?

My South is
The smell of honeysuckle
Magnolia blossoms
Chicken or ham
frying in a black iron skillet.

My South is
The sting of okra
The softness of peach fuzz
Green velvet moss
The nuzzle of a horse
Or a naked baby's bottom.
It is the shock
Of a cold creek
Born of deep underwater spring
It is the slippery, slimy salamander
Wiggling through your fingers.

My South is
The lost tribes of
Choctaw
Creek
And Cherokee.
Names they left behind
Tuscaloosa
Cahaba
Sipsey
Sylacauga
And Oneonta.

My South is in
The Heart of Dixie.
My South is

Alabama.

Rob Whitaker

A Porch: Pine Hill, Alabama

Burning heat beats down
on an unpainted porch.
A haggard man sits
waiting for heaven,
beer cans dropped
carelessly on the wood planks—
smooth, worn thin like the grass
cluttered with two by fours and rusted cars.
His calloused toes poke out
from old gray socks,
rough leather shoes sit nearby.
Horseflies buzz in the heat.

He speaks through a broken mouth
of sawmills and departed children.
The humidity suffocates;
the screened porch holds death.

Gospel music hangs in the air
breaking his already broken speech.
Shrill shrieks of children at a local VBS
bounce across the hot tin roof.
Two hours away I live in luxury—
but here sweat drips down his wrinkled forehead,
his lips forming slow words of life.

Isabelle Whitman

Lateral Movement

What to write of Alabama
whom I loved so fiercely,
then abandoned,
whose lilt and tone I mocked,
then mocked again?

This sweet grass I played on,
slept on, laid on, bled on,
left, disowned,
disavowed and defended,
worshipped and rejected.

I traded its cotton fields
for muggy swamps—
a move not up but lateral.

Joseph Whitten

Climbing Sand Mountain

Four sharp curves hug
Sand Mountain at Walker's Gap.
This autumn day
fog creeps into the first curve
caressing hickory and oak,
sourwood and October daises.
By the third curve
fog narrows the road to a ghost-lane
drawing me around the final turn
to the top. Cloud-cloaked, alone, I stop
to drink the silence
and a hundred years dissolve.
I sense the clop of horses' hooves
from valley up to mountain brow,
feel the gravel-crunch of the wagon wheels'
deliberate turning to the top.
I feel them pass before me,
those Alabama homesteaders
who made of me a mountaineer.
I recall their faces,
solemn and wrinkled,
bearded men, sunbonneted women
looking at me from black-and-white photographs.
My people, whose blood
pulses through my veins,
and I ache with love
for those I never knew.
A train cries from the valley.
The fog gives way to warming sun.
A hawk rises from a fence
and soars up into the blue expanding sky.

Miller Williams

Plain

Out of Mobile I saw a rusty Ford
fingers wrapped like pieces of rope
around the steering wheel
foxtail flapping the head of the hood
of the first thing ever
he has called his own.

Between two Bardahls
above the STP
the flag flies backwards
Go to Church This Sunday
Support Your Local Police
Post 83
They say the same thing
They say
I am not alone. [11]

II.

People Remember

Gerald Barrax

Why I am Jerald with a G and Gerry with a J:
For my Wives and Friends Who Don't Get it Right the First Time

My 17-year-old mother
Knew a G when she saw one
And wanted a G to begin my name.
Only 17 and Black
In Alabama in 1933
She knew how she wanted to name
Me. She was young and Black but not
Stupid, not uneducated.
She had been to Brooklyn, even
Had some Latin. But she said the "dumb
Peckerwood" clerk probably didn't
Know how to spell, or thought she didn't
And typed my name with a J. I don't
Know if she protested but the J
Is still on my birth certificate,
With "C" for Race, signed by Leonard V. Philps,
State Registrar of Vital Statistics
In Montgomery. Lucky for me
The times had passed when a Good Ol' Boy
Like Leonard might have decided that I
Should be a Pompey, Augustus or Cassius.

When my mother wrote my name
She did it with a G and I've been
Gerald all my life. You see
J is left-handed, and that's how
I began. In first grade
Mrs. Williams saw the birth certificate,
Gave me J for Gerry and made me
write-handed to match my mother's G.

That's all, my dears, but I've tried to make
As much of it as I can, to explain
The left-handed J inside. All his fault.

Frederick W. Bassett

A Dollhouse

It covers her grave
in the Lanett Cemetery.
Her father built it
with red brick walls,
a green-shingled roof,
windows with white awnings,
a door with a solid lock.
Perhaps the mother
chose the toys
both old and new.

I kneel at the window.
There's a framed photo
against one wall,
a doll in a brass cradle,
another on a tricycle,
two more beside a tea set
on the gray slab engraved
with name and dates
and the words
from her last birthday.

Me want it now.

Alexis Beard

All That I Am

After G.E. Lyons

I am from the stretch below
    rainbows and bluebirds
From cottonfield-covered suburban country,
gravel roads
    and one-stoplight towns
From juicy steaks, warm mashed potatoes,
And homemade pecan brownies
from the trees in grandma's backyard.

I am from a grape-bunch of middle names;
Pat, Patrick, li'l Pat; John who is Kevin
and Joanne — really Alice
I am from a tree severed and mended,
forming circles in its branches
From the rule-breaking dodge-ball thrower,
and the girl the ball hit
in the face.

I am from hot winters
And hotter summers
From the scar on the hand
where it hung on the fence
From the show-off on the motorcycle
who hit the pole in a wheelie —
and from the spectator who came running.

I am from places
    Kansas, Iowa, Alabama
  from family
    Mom, Dad, Grandma
  from experiences
    It is from all these
        That I am.

Allen Berry

The Agrarian

At age five I walked between
My grandfather and the plow,
Following growing furrows
In Alabama clay.

I understood little about the world
Seen from knee height,
I knew that he loved this land.
Through his eyes, I loved it too.

I came to understand the love
Of making things grow,
This man of contrasts
Who walked behind me.

Born to a life of farming
Coaxing life from the gentle earth
Called to a war far from home
to take the lives of strangers.

He traveled the world
On a U.S. Army ticket
Telling me once, "New Zealand
Is the Garden Spot of the world,
Next to Winfield, AL, that is."

Richard G. Beyer

To Marjorie . . . Nine Years Gone

*Whatever remembers us, finally, is enough.
If anything remembers, something is love.*
　　　　　—John Ciardi, *Minus One*

Once upon a Bloody Mary night long ago
between the remission of your myeloma
and the onset of small-cell "Big C"
into those lungs that once filled
night club nights with your songs,
we sipped those melting hours away
in a semi-deserted Birmingham lounge
listening to a struggling musician
as he whittled tender feelings raw
on the time-thread strings of an old guitar,
metering out serenades of sweet sorrow
into the bleak hours of dark mourning.

He finished "Killing Me Softly" with
"What'll I Do," "After You've Gone,"
and you gave him words of encouragement,
a sense of worth, hope for the future,
never quite saving enough for yourself.
Three men in a dark corner played cards
and each time the bearded one got lucky
he bought the house a round of drinks;
we drank free all night and thanked him
but I do not recall ever seeing his face.
Later, I wished he had been in your corner
when you finally played your last hand.

Today, I have the strangest feeling that
if I went back, they would all be there,
the guitar man, the bartender, the gambler,
some sort of Twilight Zone morality play
suspended in time and space, awaiting me.
But without a program, without your help
I'm not clever enough to grasp our roles.
I suppose the bartender must have been God,
holding things in balance, summing the tab,
but who could the rest of us be; what parts
did we play? The cold, sober daylight tells
we've both paid up; no one drinks for free. [1]

Jon Carter

Driving After Trying to Reach You, Paul

I finish a Hero Pig story
and stop at the red light
where Alabama 119 ends at the Sonic.
"So, tell me another one," Emma says.
The light turns green
and we blur by the row
of cedars that line the front
of Parkers' Drugs now boarded up,
a steady pulse, each waving in the wind
as if to say goodbye to us, Paul,
with our ice cream and twirling stools.
We pass the Wal-Mart Superstore,
the cars packed in like desert stars.

"What did you learn in school today?"
She breathes on the window
and makes a dot
with the tip of her finger.
She peeks through
her tiny creation
at the gusty world whirling by.
"There's no wind on the moon."
Odd thing to teach a five year old.
"The astronauts left a feather up there
for the next ones to find."
She breathes again
to fill the dot.
"It won't blow away."

The synthetic glove
drops the feather.
It doesn't slide this way and that but

glides
down
like an
elevator,
lands in a boot print
where it will lie

as the moon merry-go-rounds
around the earth.

Stillness brushes progress
and I find you in the friction,
old friend.

So I'm thinking about you, Paul,
grown bald, become an artist,
Heidi's e-mail tells me,
of purple and red city
scenes in evening light.
She says you ask about her husband,
"How is your partner?"

The voice on your answering machine,
though it has been twenty years,
was clearly you.

"So, tell me a Hero Pig story," Emma says,
and I begin again.
I think you will call back tonight,
maybe tomorrow.

Caitlin Channell

Old Men Chew Canned Tobacco and Call it Tasty

One more hour wasted
dancing black clock legs
tick tick
tick tick
till a timecard's stamped.
Go home to the confines
of an empty house with empty
bodies scratching
life like an ugly itch
in a town full of old, old
men broken by the strap,
buckle, switches,
leather belt, paddle
made them hardened,
southern gentlemen.
Did these wrinkles dream
beneath summer's thin sheets,
and Sunday afternoon
suppers? Trapped within
Alabama small town good
ole boys, Jack Daniels, country
music radio
tick tick
go the legs, such a small radius
of living. Long, lazy days
marked by thick brown spit
because this old man stamped
his timecard one final
Wednesday afternoon
five thirty p.m.
One more century filled
by the grumbling of old, old men.

John Curbow

Father and Son

In the Montgomery Cemetery,
father and son pose, take turns
snapping pictures in front
of twin Canadian flags furled—
and tulips curled, yellow, purple, red—
in beds at the foot
of the monument to "78 RAF Officers and Men"
who died while training near here
in World War II—"the big one"—
"the last good war," they say.

Who are they? The father is thirtyish
and flabby—the boy prepubescent
and just the same. He sits at home
among Northern frosts and plays
his game-boy. He reads books
and doesn't go outdoors. His pallid father
stares at his own version of game-boy
all day—comes home to eat
his porridge, and snores.

Are they the grandson and great
grandson of a long dead warrior—
or of one who at least wanted
to be? Like him perhaps,
they too yearn into the blue afternoon
for they know not what.

Rita Dove

Rosa

How she sat there,
the time right inside a place
so wrong it was ready.

That trim name with
its dream of a bench
to rest on. Her sensible coat.

Doing nothing was the doing:
the clean flame of her gaze
carved by a camera flash.

How she stood up
when they bent down to retrieve
her purse. That courtesy. ²

Frances R. Durham

Fishermen At Fairhope

Paint me a poem in dull gold
Just as the sky was then—
A black boat, and in it, barelegged
Two fishermen.

Shining and soundless the trawling
Of their lines in the quiet bay;
And the day burning dim behind its veils
Of gauze gray.

Give no moon, gibbous and bloody,
Not sun with a brazen glare,
But that dawn, and those mist-covered figures,
And peace there.

Vernon Fowlkes

**The Peach Speaks To Helen Gill:
Bickford Station, AL, 1899**

for Helen Gill Fowlkes, 1895 - 1984

The great, round, ripening
fruit dangled from a branch
that overhung the path to the spring.
Each day, the young girl passed it.
That peach's succulent whisper
followed her to the water's edge.
It buzzed in her ear
with an insistence that ran
circles around the grandmother's
stern forbidding. It rose
with the buzzing of flies
into the great morning
sky that blazed down on
the girl, and every fruit
hanging in the meadow.

That peach needed
no serpent's tongue. Its own
words were enough.
They rolled in her ears,
ripened in the vast
pastures she carried there.
When she slept, it nestled
its velvet fur against the soft
underside of her chin. That peach
telegraphed a landscape of dreams
into the young girl's head
and laid the world before her.

Beyond her bedroom, mysterious
animals scurried beneath the branches.
Dark water flowed
from the spring as she dreamed
the beautiful dream of the peach.

By day, under a pounding
demanding sun, she would ask
Grandma, do you think that peach is ripe, yet?
    No, Helen. A few days more.

When she could stand no more
she reached out
her hand and that peach willingly gave up
its sweet yellow flesh.
At the rail fence, she grabbed hold,
"skinned the cat" with delight
over the sweetness of stolen fruit.
Juice ran into her nose, streamed
in with the fury
of Divine Retribution. She was sure
it was the fire of Hell. She remembered
her grandmother's words,
the Old Man's fiery preaching, dropped
the half-eaten peach in the dirt.
With her sewing box, she huddled
on the porch swing and sewed
buttons on little clothes.

She had eaten forbidden fruit
and she knew now what
it meant to be naked.

Diane Garden

Portrait of My Father and Me with the *USS Alabama*

I keep returning to a memory of my father
when mother let me take him to lunch
when she stayed behind to play with Hannah
at their hotel. From the deck overlooking
the Tensaw River, we watched two men
in kayaks with strong arms lift the current
and disappear like orange and red
streaks at sunset. I didn't have to attack
mother and unleash his fury—attention
that connected him to me, that threatened
like a frayed wire. I gave in to the wind
and sun, to cattails swaying feathery flags,
to a border of rushes across the waterway
with pale golden tops and dark stems
like a row of paintbrushes with tips drying
in the sun. I asked him questions
whose answers wouldn't boomerang
back to our family war zone. I listened
to stories about his stint as a civilian
at Pearl Harbor—days welding
ships in the sun, nights at the canteen
chatting with buddies, dancing with island
girls to "Boogie Woogie Bugle Boy,"
or watching *For Me and My Gal.*
As he leaned over the table and poured
more wine for me, his hand brushed
mine, and I looked up and smiled.
I hope this moment keeps on replacing
past portraits. We're together at the table,
with the *USS Alabama* in the distance,
with its grey tiers and stilled torpedoes.

Faye Gaston

War Widow, 1863

I own an old original tin-type
of a woman, dignified, unbowed—
my great-grandmother, a soldier's wife,
soon a widow when the states went to war.
Did she ever wonder what he fought for?
Were her thin lips soft as a southern breeze?
Her dreams like clouds in Alabama skies?
Her work-worn hands show a life of labor.
Was her grief or hard times the greater foe?
Was that a whisper of a smile to tease
those who read heartbreak in her deep-set eyes?

Gail Gehlken

Alabama women

like my mother
know how to open each hour,
fill its seconds and minutes
with sweetened juices and pulp
of memories

like packing mason jars
with hot, spiced pear relish
before capping with sealing flaps
and gold twist rings

to hold a luscious taste of August
for a cold December day.

Anne George

This Day I Give My Father
October 29, 1929

It is Black Thursday but
he doesn't know that. He
sits on the bluff over Mobile Bay
and thinks how October light
turns things golden, especially my mother
in her yellow dress who walks
at the edge of the water
and bends awkwardly to wash a shell.
Feeling his gaze, she looks up,
shields her eyes, waves.
Tomorrow he will learn of loss,
of defeated men dropping from buildings.
But this day I give my father
a warm ripe tomato to bite into,
goldenrod lining the shell road,
pelicans skimming the water,
and my mother looking up to wave,
sun bleached hair shining, her hand
pressed against her huge belly. [3]

Mary Halliburton

The Legacy

Raised in the projects of Montgomery
Ruby held my hand when I was small,
gave my family food. She taught me
to read pain in faces
and how a gentle hand made them smile.

We tilled the soil,
watched vegetables and flowers grow.
"Plants are like people," she said.
"You have to get the weeds away, give love."

The poor came to her door.
Ruby met them with smiles,
shared food, money, and clothes.
She helped the sick and sang at church.
She praised the Lord, said amen
louder than any of us. No one made fun.
She lived her religion.

I worried when Ruby died, because
she had no family. I was wrong.
Everyone she'd fed, clothed
and loved were her family.
The church filled to capacity, overflowed
to grounds and street.
I wondered what I'd do without her.

Then I saw a lost child
and held out my hand.

Ralph Hammond

Molly and Josephus of Upper Alabama

In early pioneer days
old woman Molly Hornbuckle
lived with her grouchy old man Josephus
on the top side of Sand Mountain
in Upper Alabama.

Across the long years
she hated the task
of scrubbing floors
and washing windows.

And to her old man's
griping and whining complaints
about the messy house,
she had a ready answer:

"Tarnation, Josephus,
cleaning house ain't
nary a thang
but rearranging dirt!"

Peter Huggins

John Beecher in Birmingham

I was an accident, you know.
My parents didn't want children.
They were too busy: L.T. making
Money hand over fist at Tennessee
Coal and Iron, Mother reading
On the Chautauqua circuit up north.
No home life, I can tell you that.

Mother tried to make up for it at Christmas,
When I was down from Cornell.
She got me a date with a girl
Of good family and social connection,
As Mother so bluntly put it.
I didn't want to go with the girl.
When Mother insisted, I shaved

My head bald. Mother didn't bat an eye
When she introduced me to the girl.
The poor girl didn't know
What to make of me. I suppose
I looked freakish to her,
Like one of L.T.'s workers emerging
From that dark mill of his.

L.T. didn't appreciate my antics.
He mumbled something about the mind
Being its own place. Mother said
He had a gift for picking
Phrases out of context, a gift
That I seem to have inherited.
My fire's in the valley: all I see is me. [4]

Ramona L. Hyman

Mind Chatter: For Rosa Parks

Her name: Rosa Parks
The day: one
The year: 1955
The month: December
The place: Montgomery, Alabama

Rosa: she tired she say
She tired when she board the bus
Walked down the center isle—tired,
Sat (in the first of the last ten pairs of seats)
Tired

Fable go:
black folks couldn't ride up front
black folks seats in back a the bus
they just like a bugs
sit 'em in the back of the bus so,
tired, tired Rosa—she sit down in the back of the bus

Bus got crowded
Driver tell black folks sitting
in the first of the last ten pairs of seats
to stand—"make it light on themselves" stand

Rosa ain't stand
(ain't make it light)

Fable go:
King say:
"Rosa Parks anchored (anchored)
by accumulated indignities of
days gone by, the boundless
aspirations of generations yet unborn."

King say:
"Rosa Parks a victim (a victim)
Of the forces of destiny."

King say:
"When the cup of endurance runs over,
The human personality cries out."

Rosa Parks, she cry out, she cry
For the black African brought on
A slave-ship—packed like sardines in stale water
She cry, she cry out so
I can sit on the bus
She cry; she get arrested
She get finger printed
She quiet

Fable go:
Nobody know the trouble she see
Nobody know but Jesus

Rosa Parks tired; black folks tired
She found guilty on 5 December 1955
Black folks tired; they start the boycott
Cause they tired
My mama tired, too
She in the boycott
Yo mama, yo daddy in it, too
They walk. They don't catch the bus
They crawl; they don't catch the bus
They walk. For over a year;
They go to court, keep
Going to court

The court get some sense

Fable go:
June 1956 Montgomery Court say:
Back of the bus sitting for black folk ain't right.
November 1956 United States Supreme Court say:
back of the bus sitting for black folk ain't right

Rosa Parks stopped walking
Black folks stopped walking
White folks stopped walking, too

Rosa Parks get some rest
Black folks get some rest
White folks—they get some rest, too

Rodney Jones

Two Girls At The Hartselle, Alabama, Municipal Swimming Pool

Too much of the country in their walk—
as though each struggled
against a tree at the center of her body,
or all the bare feet were shoes

that didn't fit, poverty in every step,
in every move, deliberate
as footsteps in plowed fields,
through clots of local boys, up

slipper rungs to the high board,
their bodies oiled, flipping away
casually the menthol cigarettes,
tossing back their bleached hair,

both twelve or thirteen years old:
like old houses, like mothers
pitched forward into the wind,
entering the cold, strange waters. [5]

Penne Laubenthal

Alabama Clay: Mentone, 1989
for David

With hands as hard as clay
   he gently strokes
      the chieftain's face
as if to trace
   a trail of tears.

I watch his eyes fill
   and my love spills
      in rivers
for this man who
   lifts the sculptured bust
      and hugs it to his
flannelled bosom
   like a child.

I smile
   and search our meager purse,
and when I find enough,
we join hands and
   journey down the mountain with our treasure—
      his
         and
            mine.

Karen Middleton

The Snow of `88

A rare Alabama snow and children too young to remember
    any whiteness of earth revel in its chilly enchantment.
Their delighted cries beckon me to plunge through drifts
    of memory piled high outside my window.

Knee-high boots found in the workshop still covered
    in last spring's creek mud fit snugly.
Green rubber reminders of perfect love wear the red clay
    legacy of an absent adventurer.

The creek-wader walks single file within me, leaving rusty
    imprints in my snowy ones.
His tracks in mine. I create him again to feel the cold
    and lick the ice from a frozen mitten.

Life, then, goes on: spring melts winter's tracks, summer bakes
    hard the earth and too soon fall fades to winter.
But sometimes a Southern snow yields up adolescent evidence
    of life-giving, blood-red clay.

Claire W. Mikkelsen

Soul Brothers?

Double-wild he was—our own Hank Williams.
Wild on drugs and whiskey, but also
Alabama country-man wild.

I can see him out in Hollywood
hat tilted down just above his eyes
and feet up on a producer's desk.
Enigmatic, aloof and wary.

Like I can picture federal judge Frank Johnson
sitting in church muttering "It's all a pack of lies!"
Two different (yet similar) country people.

Their own men, not easy to decipher,
rich in complexity, tension and spark.

The real articles.

Shayla Mollohan

Enough: The Wake You Wanted, Lake Guntersville, 1993
for Tom Boles

I wondered aloud if this would be enough to feed them.
Like "All dressed up and nowhere to go," he would have said.
Where had the morning dawned? Impossible noon...

Mourners look at the deliciousness of the table — the crowder
    peas, the speckled butterbeans
boasting a meaty hambone, fried potatoes and cut corn shucked
    from the silks of summer.
Chicken sweats beneath the plastic wrap, this bloated morning
    attendance, uncensorable.
Required. What is the time?

His hands rivered his age, oddly folded neatly across stapled ribs.
Take it easy, Daddy.
Hours ago the struggle was on, eyes focused on nothing living.
    It's all about the journey.
He was his destination. The candle wax already liquefying, wicks
    floated beyond
their brass banks in a bed of carnations, yellow roses and mums.
    He hated cut
flowers. "No good to us now," he'd say. Once in a box, an urn, too
    late.

He cleaned fish better than anyone. We got him an electric knife
    for Christmas.
Filleting made simple: chop off the tail, chop off the head and
    pull out the guts. Pull off
the skin. Perfect white meat, fissured nicely at the prongs of a
    plastic table fork
when done.

We ate at picnic tables on the screened porch, North Salty smells
    wafting up
to us from the limestone garden, abbreviated by the water
    and thorn brush.
You could not know what it was like to love you. To be loved by
    you.
It wasn't in him to know, then.
Too hard.

No ritual could have made this more digestible, more lovely to
    fry up.
Instead, he held on to me just a little longer that one day. The day
    I keep with me, framed
in the soul of me like Jesus and my husband's water-green eyes.
In some places,
beauty survives forever.

You look really good in that tie, Daddy. "I looked good in almost
anything. . ." I pass out the plates. A bass rises from the water
    to show
his young white belly in the sun, the splash indiscernible.

Carl Morton

To a Neighbor Who Knew
Vestavia Hills, Alabama

How precious were those days toward April's dying
though other springs will pass—but not for him,
who never breathed sweet March without soul sighing,
who ever viewed each flower's diadem

as resurrection's crown from winter death,
each miracle of grass returning green
proof evident there *is* no dying breath
for those with faith to see the great unseen.

All flowering of nature for his wreath,
we harken to this symphony of air
and all these stirring cosmic things beneath,
consign the living to the living's care,

defer to sanctuaries of this sod
and let Joe go. He is at Spring with God.

Cheryl Moyer

The Secret of Old Age
One week in Greene County

With a rusty bucket in hand
in worn overalls as patched
and thin as his shoes he
walked along the side of the
road... He was 74 years old
and carrying fresh cut greens
to his daughter's house 13 miles away.

Minnie who was 69 was
running off to work to take
care of an "old woman" of 91.

Sarah was 82 and her mom 99.
They sewed quilts for a living
and were preparing for the
mother's 100th birthday party
soon to come.

I stopped to ask directions
from Georgia who was hanging
clothes on the line, she said
she was 105. She had cleaned
houses all her life.

So I asked her the Alabama
secret for old age:

Was it the slow living in the warm sun?
Was it the clean air, or pure water?
Was it good food prepared by loving hands?

She smiled and said "Yes, it's all that"

"But mostly . . . it's the hard work".

Then she hung another shirt
up on the line.

Michael Pollick

Modern Cuts for Modern Men

His father ran the power company like a cheap Swiss watch,
as the last of the cuts poured out blood and Mad Dog—
mama's precious blue-eyed drunk lay gutted and silenced,
gutted and silenced on Huntsville city property.

Olan Mills had no idea what was once captured on film,
Tom and Vivian and two small ideas for boys;
each looking so bright and sober that morning, the combs
finding no reluctance, no resistance, no defiance.

One would grow to be his father's waking dream—a Marine
pulled and taut and inspection-ready, drawing his service
revolver so smoothly one might never feel the sting.

The other son would not appear in any more wallet-sized pictures,
nor would he ever agree to pass the plate in church again.
This son would fail to keep his promises to God and country,
mired in too much piss and Wild Irish Rose to be gracious.

His father would identify the body in his own sweet time,
but the police already held a homeless man responsible;
joggers found the boy sprawled over some battered suitcases,
his one acceptable arm already pointed towards home.

David Pratt

The Gift That's Unexpected

What about love? she says
She looks at me across the shrimp and oysters
We meet like this, every few months, to talk theology
I bite on something hard, and hope it's not a broken tooth

She looks at me across the shrimp and oysters
It's March: the southern air is soft and warm
I bite on something hard, and hope it's not a broken tooth
Along the causeway, pelicans dive for fish

It's March: the southern air is soft and warm
Across the bay, the Alabama looms
Along the causeway, pelicans dive for fish
I tongue the object from my mouth

Because she's here, the day is radiant
Between my fingers is a tiny pearl
The word made flesh, she says
The gift that's unexpected is the best

Between my fingers is a tiny pearl
We meet like this, every few months, to talk theology
The gift that's unexpected is the best
What about love? she says.

Morton Prouty

Valedictory

To Henry Grady Richards on the occasion of his retirement after forty-four years as principal of Gilbert School, Florence, Alabama

A few words of truth, but the truth that they told
Hurried straight to the heart like an arrow shot through,
And a child held the truth to be dearer than gold,
And the man in him learned what it meant to be true.

A bright plume of courage, worn high on the crest
Of a man who dared live by the code that he gave,
And a child learned how he could stand up with the best,
And the man in him learned what it meant to be brave.

A firm gentle hand, lending strength to the right,
Laid restraint on the bully, rebuking the wrong,
And a child learned to know in what cause he must fight,
And the man in him learned what it meant to be strong.

A mind, reading nature with wonder and awe,
Sought for meaning in everything God had designed,
And the child found new meaning in nature's old law,
And the man learned how learning gives wings to the mind.

A heart full of love for the children he knew;
They are legion, the children his love would enroll;
And the child learned the meaning of love as he grew,
And the man learned how love can give wings to the soul.

Pat Schneider

One Day In Mobile
for Sue Walker

We walk behind your old dog
on the rain-wet avenue. Talk
poetry and azaleas. Alabama
slow and sleepy in the rain.

You warn me not to step aside
to touch a blossom. You say
even the dog knows
not to mess with rattlers.

Telling stories, we walk
through pages of our lives:
your hurricanes,
my twisters.

You built your house of stone—
strong against inevitable wind
and I bend into who I am
from cyclone circumstances.

We have survived, and that's
an art in any state. It helps
to have an old dog, azaleas,
poems, and rain. Thank you.

Thomi Sharpe

Delta`s Blues

The Captain, troubled on this leaden winter day,
looks out from his window, the sights bring him down.
Suddenly dark, he pushes himself up, draws in a breath
and drags the water with him out of Mobile Bay.

He leaves Delta lying naked on the killing floor
stripped of her long blue dress, legs wide.
Seagrass, like stretch-marks ripple her tan skin.
Her graying hair hangs limp from the bones of Water Tupelo.
Unruly patches of broom sedges sprout in embarrassing places.
Her once pleasing curves, fuller,
sagging, slightly rounded, rolling over the edge of the road
freckled with the crab-traps and beer bottles of the night before.

She's given birth to ungrateful children.
Double breasted cormorants, black robes flapping up
      court house steps,
long-billed curlews picking over all night seafood buffets,
winter ducks with yellowing hair squatting in steno pools,
purple coated grackles puffing out their chests, noses in the air
their electric screeches of self importance like the hum
      of florescent lights,
slump shouldered red tailed hawks skulking in parking lots
      kicking the gong,
laughing gulls, still brown, playing dozens in the sand
      at her feet.

The Captain turns his back to her, how could she let herself go?
He remembers when she was beautiful. A real biscuit roller.
Ramblin' roadhouses, juke joints, and shabby hotels
      have taken their toll.
He loops his arm round a long legged canary in a white dress,
lights up his cigar sending out a thick cloud of fog,

"Doe, you might want to cover yourself," he says as he goes on
    up the line.
And Delta cries. Large wet tears fall on her lap rolling in rivulets
    over her asphalt knees.
The sky reels outraged, booming in disapproval.

A mixed flock like doubt swarms around her head, descending,
a noisy black blanket covering her
shimmering with threads of copper and gold.
The sun looks down, spills lemon through the swamp chestnut
    oak trees.
The golden child brushes away the scratching blanket
    before shyly climbing in bed,
covering Delta with rose-colored caresses and tangerine kisses.
A dozen white pelicans rise like fresh clean sheets,
flapping in the gray winter wind.

Jim Simmerman

Child's Grave, Hale County, Alabama

Someone drove a two-by-four
through the heart of this hard land
that even in a good year
will notch a plow blade worthless,
snap the head off a shovel,
or bow a stubborn back.
He'd have had to steal
the wood from a local mill
or steal, by starlight, across
his landlord's farm, to worry
a fencepost out of its well
and lug it the three miles home.
He'd have had to leave his wife
asleep on a corn shuck mat,
leave his broken brogans
by the stove, to slip outside,
quiet as sin, with the child
bundled in a burlap sack.
What a thing to have to do
on a cold night in December,
1936, alone
but for a raspy wind
and the red, rock-ridden dirt
things come down to in the end.
Whoever it was pounded
this shabby half-cross
into the ground must have toiled
all night to root it so:
five feet buried with the child
for the foot of it that shows.
And as there are no words
carved here, it is likely that
the man was illiterate,

or addled with fatigue,
or wrenched simple-minded
by the one simple fact.
Or else the unscored lumber
driven deep into the land
and the hump of busted rock
spoke too plainly of his grief:
forty years laid by and still
there are no words for this. [6]

Julie Suk

Whoever They Call Mad

the exact name slips
Miss Elise   Miss Fanny   Miss Alleta Jane
whoever they call mad
a compulsive walker
every morning at eight
the same crepe dress
frazzled as moss
ribbon at the throat
beaded bag
and circling her head
the wide-wheeled galaxy
of an infinitely purple hat
every morning at eight
down the crumbling steps
past columned houses
infested by glories
snarled back on their seed
every morning dogs
railed against chains
dogs at her heels
dogs at the drugstore   hardware   trolley
dogs sprawled at the feet of old cronies
don't pay her no mind
she don't bother nobody
every morning to the dock
past honky-tonks latticed porches
whores rocking their grievances
back uptown to the square
three times around through pigeon flocks
scattered lord knows where
the route lost until five
when she showed for a tray
whoever they call kind

everyday the same
rarely spoke
never complained
walked as they said
to her grave
we still look for the ghost
the dogged
the mad
crazed to tear loose
Miss Elise   Miss Fanny   Miss Aleta Jane [7]

Kathleen Thompson

Men Going Fishing

Up before daylight, shaking
younger ones, stretching away sleep,
they convene silently in the kitchen.
Old hair is spiked with restless sleep,
as unruly as they had been as teenagers.
Buttons and zippers are at odds
from dressing in dark bedrooms;
they are as awkward here without women
as if they were asking for directions,
admitting somehow they were lost.

Each opens and stares into cabinets,
in separate brown studies, searching,
ripping box tops from cereal,
toasting a bagel or bread, groping
inside the refrigerator for butter,
all making breakfast choices;
some stacking sandwiches to take,
more than enough, just in case;
relatives passing shoulder to shoulder
like strangers shopping for food.

The oldest, an unlikely fisher now,
limps in late hurrying, more eager
to go than his arthritic knees, eager
to repeat tales of how things used to be,
stories the grandsons are too young
to remember, how Gulf Shores
had more fishing boats than tourists,
when there was no limit on red snapper,
grouper, or amberjack and boats groaned
from the reckless gluttony of each catch.

A younger one measures sound
with his face following his evening
at Live Bait, the lines cutting deeper
with each gurgle of the 30-cup pot;
as deliberate in closing a cabinet

as if he were handling fine crystal,
he seeks the simple treasure of a mug;
he knows just where his wife keeps them
at home, but where are they hidden here,
here in this kitchen of moving men.

Sue Brannan Walker

The Nature of Dreams: The Making Of a Naturalist
for Edward O. Wilson

Take an Alabama boy with dreams
and let him wander as he will
to seek secrets in the swamp.
Let him feel mud squish
between his toes, wade into streams,
dive into rivers, and find how it is
to grab a water snake, as green
as innocence, stare into its yellow eyes,
mark its frozen half-smile and as it stretches
along fringing weeds,
revere it like an ancient mariner,
bless it, even in fear.

Take a boy who rises at 3:00 a.m.
before the sun contemplates
the circuit it will travel, long before
the plush first breath of dawn
and give him a bike and a job.
Tell him there is nothing
he can't do—like delivering 420 *Mobile Registers*
before grits and eggs, before breakfast at 7:30
and a long day at school.

Take a boy who learns how to stoop
and bend, who learns that obstructions
are lessons in how to change direction.
A small thing like an ant can be huge,
can be authority, can make an entomologist
world-renowned.

Take a boy who discovers
magic and mystery in a sea nettle
swimming bay waters, in an ant's
mastery of construction. *Microwildernesses
exist in a handful of soil. The trip of a lifetime
is around the trunk of a single tree.*
This is testimony, is promise, is the way
to love the world and honor it,
to honor ourselves, who above all else
learn to dwell in a place and do no harm. [8]

Jake Adam York

Walt Whitman in Alabama

Maybe on his way to Gadsden,
Queen City of the Coosa,
to speak with the pilots and inland sailors,
to cross the fords Jackson ran with blood
or meet the mayor who
bought the ladies' favors with river quartz,
maybe east from some trip west to see
or returning north from New Orleans
or just lost in those years after The War
as legend has it, after the bannings,
when he'd grown tired of puffs and plates,
after he'd grown the beard and begun
to catch things there he had to walk off
or sing unwritten, maybe when the open road
opened on mockingbirds two and two
no one knows, though the stories have him here
recapturing Attalla, shaking poems from his hair
on the steps of local churches. Maybe
it was the end of many letters, the last
of hospital days, another sleight
to make his hand come alive
when he couldn't bring some Southron home.
I see him there remembering his poems,
his back to the door, singing
out to the garden of the world,
the tropical spring of pine and jasmine,
how wondrous it was the pent-up river
washed to green their farms, the creeks swole
with mountain dew to sprout the corn,
herbage of poke and collard,
spinach and bean, to wash the roots
of every leaf to come. But more
I wonder what he did not say,
whether the doors were closed on the room

where none thought Jesus ever naked,
whether he went down Gadsden's Broad
to the bluff where a hundred years thence
someone fabled a child lost from the arms
of his hispanic mother and almost saved
by a cop who brought from his pocket
a shirt's worth of proof before the woman
vanished with her English, before the psychics
started rowing down the channel
to listen for the baby's dreams—all years after
the whorehouses, the fires, Reconstruction
and true religion came, after Whitman said his piece
and left the county to its mayors,
its wars and local dramas, Broad Street
and its theatres to opening and closing
and being torn down to photograph and rumor
where Vaudeville variety traveled
in those years before the world became real
and history stilled, before the damns stalled
the yearly flood that washed the roots
and made new fields from catfish and shit
and the mountain dead, before
the sun in the tassels was wormed to shine,
before shine dried into the hills
with the snakes, the poetry, the legend.
I imagine him here in the different city,
bathing in the yellow light as the river slips
beneath the bridge, flickering like a candle
or like the body or like the bodies
lit up with gasoline and beer, tremble of taillights,
while the statue of the Civil War heroine
points fingerless down Broad, down the stream
of headlamps and embers of burning weed,
a congregation in which his secrets and his song
would be unwelcome, though he slake
some secret thirsts, his orotund voice
tune our ears to the river's whisper,
a baby cradled in branches
deep beneath the bridge.

Its ribs filter the Coosa's brown.
Its arms raise the crops.
And every night it whispers the town
in some new forgotten tongue.

III.

Music Remembers

Leonard Aldes

Oh Alabama, I'll Remember You

I was born upon your soil
A richness hardly well deserved,
And with stars ablaze across the night
I took my place with you.

Oh Alabama how you touched my soul,
Your auburn hills and tapestries,
Your rivers deep, yet calm and smooth,
Here I could be free.

So perfect lay your earth and shores
Such grace in you as it should be,
And winds so soft as if a kiss
That whispers through the trees.

And beneath your deep blue canopy
I recall as if but yesterday,
Stretched pearls of white, your fields—so pure,
Like arms stretched out to pray.

And when dusk set still upon your bays
The heavens glowed with golden spires
That danced and gleamed on oceans vast
And lit your nights on fire.

Oh Alabama you have given much,
No other place but could I be,
To the fates I say, "Thank you, I'm blessed,"
Your spirit burns in me.

And though the years have marked their time
No regrets have I of my time spent
With my true love, my dearest friend,
Oh Alabama, I'll remember you.

Jake Berry

Alabama Dust

"The moon is just a blue eyed witch
with the devil in her soul,"
so the old man said
and walked on down the road.
I never saw him again,
but the story went around
that he fell for a blue-eyed girl
and caught the last bus out of town.

It was a dark day in the valley
the day I met you.
You were a long tall Sally,
lord, you played me for a fool.
If I could find the way out,
where I came in,
I'd hit the ground running,
I'd be gone with the wind.

I'm gonna pack my bags
and get on the bus
bound for Birmingham
in that Alabama dust.

I brought a bouquet of flowers
and set them on your window sill.
When you sent your boy around for money
I gave him all that I could steal.
Now the heartbroken sky
turns the stars to tears
and I'd bet my soul to a dollar
you'll be wanting them.

I'm gonna pack my bags
and get on the bus
bound for Birmingham
in that Alabama dust.

Early last week
in her Sunday-go-to-meeting dress
they laid sister Mary in the ground
for a long, long rest.
You see, it ain't about what's real,
it ain't about which god you trust,
it's how you disappear
in that Alabama dust.

I'm gonna pack my bags
and get on the bus
bound for Birmingham
in the Alabama dust.

Langston Hughes

Daybreak in Alabama

When I get to be a composer
I'm gonna write me some music about
Daybreak in Alabama
And I'm gonna put the purtiest songs in it
Rising out of the ground like a swamp mist
And falling out of heaven like soft dew.
I'm gonna put some tall tall trees in it
And the scent of pine needles
And the smell of red clay after rain
And long red necks
And poppy colored faces
And big brown arms
And the field daisy eyes
Of black and white black white black people
And I'm gonna put white hands
And black hands and brown and yellow hands
And red clay earth hands in it
Touching everybody with kind fingers
And touching each other natural as dew
In that dawn of music when I
Get to be a composer
And write about daybreak
In Alabama.

Hank Lazer

Banjo

oh susan   oh
susanna   don't you
cry for me

oh susan   how
not to let
world circumstance become

a personal lament
for i've gone
to alabama   &

the children the
small ones how
do we get

from that to
this   to alabama
with a banjo

on my knee
to sing an
indirect changing blues

Melissa Morphew

Alabama Afternoon: A Love Song

The pleasure-ache of an ordinary day,
like summer, always at the edge of breath, a greenness,
sugar-light, syruped-sun, afternoon hush—
a sleeping porch, a bed,
white curtains bleached blue with shadow,
a galvanized tub, her bath, water washing over her body,
the silk of soap-wet hair, a rough towel,
a yellow dress; she stretches her legs and there
is no pleasure beyond this, beyond her muscle's
tense, release, the heat, dampness of her hair
upon her neck, silence of cicada-song,
pollened-thrum of honey bees, willow leaves
filigreed against the blinds,
undernoise of her heart as she drowses,
flower-dreaming each stubborn petal of nasturtium,
Persian lilac, orange rosettes of cucumber vine,
and when she wakes — green pears on a clear glass plate,
yellow cheese, thick-crusted bread, dandelion wine,
all of these, all of these . . .

John T. Morris

Rondeau to William Christopher Handy

Who first committed the words and music of jazz
and southern spirituals to immortal print. Before
Handy, none of America's greatest contribution
to world music had ever been published.

The blues were born in Handy's heart
From throbbing, drumming Congo art,
That drove the Lalique fog away
And warmed like jungle astral ray
His soul and voodoo counterpart.

Handy was no brash upstart,
He studied Handel and Mozart,
And it was not through idle play
The blues were born.

He took the jungle art apart,
And wrote it on a music chart
That played from Beale street to Broadway
In music hall and cabaret
And with this prelusory star
The blues were born. [1]

Richard Scott Nokes

Bluegrass Bards of Alabama

The bluegrass bards unpack their bows
preparing for the surprise party
for the fellow who teaches my daughter fiddle.
The lodge in Luverne is poorly lit,
which is just as well; the walls are
slick with grease, slightly slimy,
the room ragged. Feeling run-down,
I am tired. Eying my wife,
I send her a psychic message, suggesting
with my look that I'd like to leave early.
She knows that look, and nods to me.
A good wife, she gets the message.
Sighing, I settle into my seat.

The sentries at the door don't see
the guest of honor go up the back.
He creeps in through the kitchen
and peers over the porcelain counter, puzzled.
"Calvin!" someone shouts, and everyone cries
out "Happy birthday!" in a hurried, weak shout.
The instruments ignite in his honor.

My wife wields her bow like a weapon,
aggressively attacks her fiddle as an enemy.
"Boil the Cabbage Down" is bold and frantic;
"Ashokan Farewell," though, is as an old friend,
the bow kisses out the notes, caressing the strings.
I can't really hear her, however, only see;
A variety of voices drown out her violin:
music from mandolins, guitars, fiddles, and more.
The sounds sneak up on me. Surprised, I realize

Nashville's newest idols are nothing next to these.
The crowd playing is from the countryside,
rural people, ridiculed as rednecks;
the likelihood any of them ever had a lesson
seems slim. Their instruments sing
with power that practice alone can't produce.

The hall-sitters grew out of the ground, and their guitars
and fiddles flowered on them, Dixie's fruit.
Bluegrass here is native-born, in the blood,
in the sap and the soil, in the sons and their souls.
I have been holding back my heart,
imagining that my identity as an interloper,
my Yankee rearing rending me unique,
culturally separate — the carpetbagger in the corner.
No more. I'm moved by these musicians,
warriors of the wiregrass. Nothing more withheld,
I realize a little root has reached down from me,
and sips from the soil, an adopted son.

Jack Pendarvis

Hank Williams

At twenty nine? He died at twenty-nine?
It scares me now more than Mozart. Not that Hank
Had ever walked the starry razor line
Or drunk the angel dew that Mozart drank.
For art, let's clearly call it blasphemy
To mention all the songs he ever wrote,
His whole blue world of highs and misery,
Beside one Mozart phrase, if not one note.
Yet Mozart was a youngster drunk on day
While Hank was old, his heart a caved-in sun,
And I will not feel ignorant to say
That in his last mass Mozart had begun,
Through bars and broken beams, to barely sight
The light Hank always saw, that dying light.

Margaret Britton Vaughn

Hank

They say he walks the lost highway
Searching for back road taverns
Where people drop their coins
Into the poor man's psychiatrist
Who talks in grooves about
Cheating hearts and lonesome cries.
His lanky frame holds a picture
Of a pale soul, broken heart,
Sad voice and a mind packed
with tortured memories
that all subtracted from his life
but added to his genius.
He was a plain poet, the kind
People were drawn to
By pictures he developed
Just for them.
He sleeps during the day
While people stand over him
And read his name
Chiseled in stone.
At night he stands
Over people and sees
His words chiseled in
Concrete images
On people's souls.
He should be getting up now;
The honkytonks are coming alive.

Eugene Walter

The Night Concert At Dog River

Thunder in the night,
Rain with it bringing;
All through the storm
The crickets keep singing.

The river has risen,
The reeds are enflooded.
The young bay saplings
All denuded.

But music continues
In reeds, in the thickets;
Katydids, bull frogs,
The locusts and crickets.

But sweetest of all,
Full of sorrowing wonder,
The sad sleepy tree-frog
Cries through the thunder.

William J. Wilson

Old Bookem

When Old Bookem plays the fiddle
at First Monday, there's a plaint
deeper than he owns hiding in the notes
like a mockingbird lost in the treetops.
Uncertain, it recalls the solitude of lean men
in a near-empty land of fragrant cedars,
cool hollows and springs where hills beyond hills
recede westward to the mythic Mississippi.
Perhaps it's the land itself singing its song
through Bookem, lonesome, modal and minor,
green like the West was never green
and rough with outcrops or soft with mist,
forever arguing against the fence and plow.
Something survives in the music, ownerless
and indelible as their ancient surnames
misspelled and scattered across Alabama.

C. W. Zoan

Acrostic Hymn to Huntsville

Here in Upper Alabama, in the Tennessee River Valley, your city—
    home to William Bankhead, Tallulah Bankhead,
        John Sparkman, Jan Davis—
Unique from its beginning, its Big Springs, a
Natural voice that allured John Hunt in 1805.
Then on to become the first incorporated town in Alabama,
       to host our State's first constitutional convention,
       to become the State's first capital,
       to cotton and antebellum homes, and
           textile mills—Lincoln and Merrimack—
    to watercress capital of the world,
    to Rocket City.
Symphonies, drama, musicals, chorus, Big Spring Jam, Panoply,
    Poetry, Museums, Libraries combine in a
Venue where engineers, scientists, educators, musicians escape the
    complexities of a life,
Involved with missiles, rockets and space at Redstone Arsenal,
    and in
League with educators and students at UAH, A&M University,
    and Oakwood College to
Learn more of the unutterable mysteries of the universe, its vast,
    misty reaches, with
Everyone drawing together to focus on new horizons, to create
    other uniqueness.

IV.

Seasons Remember

Jane Allen

Cotton Pickin', 1953

for *Billy Tom*

Fall in Alabama meant cotton pickin' time.
Mama and Daddy kept
all us young'uns out of school and sent us
to the ripened fields.

Burs pricked my thin fingers,
blood spurted on the white balls.
As sweat saturated my eyes,
as dog flies plunged into my hair,
as gnats swarmed round my ears,
as sunrays branded my skin,
as horseflies descended on my hoe,
as spit splattered on my face,
I retched in pure disgust.

At the end of the day, we dragged
our achin' bones home,
sipped cool well water,
and collapsed on the shady porch boards,
dreading yet another dawn
of pickin' cotton.

J. William Chambers

Farewell to a Garden: Athens, Alabama, Autumn 2002

*Did only softly stealing hours
There close the peaceful lives of flowers?*
—*Wordsworth*

Late Dortmunds linger
in disembodied ecstasy;
remnants of Stargazer lilies peer
through grasping autumn wisteria;
a scraggly patch
where Joe-Pye weed,
coral bells and calla lilies
departed long ago;
two clumps of Lilies-of-the-Nile,
now death-devoted;
Love-Lies Bleeding,
languid in its white-crusted pot;
rampant mints here;
strangling ivy there.

Neglect should never have covered
your glories . . . yet, it's there,
rough-hewing all symmetry
Steve had planned
over the past two decades—
you the great challenger,
we the celebrants
of your mysticism.
Should not this venture
      have come,
then, to some great spiritual
      unfolding?

Perhaps . . . but did not we grow
old together? Tired and weary?
Sick and discouraged?

Steve and I take the path
by Cecile Brünner,
unhappiest rose of all this year.
We do not look back
when we hear the last pear fall. [1]

Reese Danley-Kilgo

One Alabama Spring

Driving down the country road,
we wound around small hills,
across fields, over a shaky wooden bridge.
Finally we found the farm: old house
weathered, nestled under pecan trees,
wood smoke rising from chimney
of gray-brown native stone.
We had heard there were guineas
for sale here, and hoped to buy a few
of these strange checkered fowl,
because they were a part of a childhood
too many years, too many miles
from this day, this May morning,
far away from a mother who
died too soon, too young.
In cardboard carton, punched
with holes, six guinea chicks
chirk and cheep as we drive home.
My mother called them keets, and I
never thought to ask her why.
Mother, I wonder where you learned
this rare word, and why you were so fond
of this rare bird. There are many,
more important, questions left
unasked, unanswered.
This little flock of guinea fowl,
are for my children, two little girls
who will never know you, except through
the few memories I have of you and me
scattering corn on the ground,
for guineas roosting high
in chinaberry trees,
hiding
in chinaberry leaves.

Wade Hall

A Call to Winter Uses
In Memoriam, WHH, 1910-68

Do not close your eyes today, my mother,
Because my father left last night.
There is light still for joy
And things to be done.
The warm fields are yet green;
The sun is bright on the empty barn.
The watermelons show sweet promise
Among the deep green vines
And the scuppernongs will soon turn golden
On the ancient arbor your father built.
There will be food enough and wine for supper.

The sweet potato house needs filling
Or there will be no pies for Christmas.
The sugar cane must be cut and stripped
and its juice rendered into syrup
Or there will be no Christmas candy.
The pecans are raw inside their hulls
(Only canker worms bring them down so early);
We must be patient and pick them from the brown grass
To liven up the Christmas cakes.
Chinquipins and chestnuts are filling out
      in secret places over the ridge:
They must be found or there will be no Christmas nuts.

My father could not wait till September
And the gathering in.
He plowed the land,
Roofed the house and crib and barn
And warned that ready crops soon go to waste,
Undoing toil and time.

Now the cotton planted in the month of hope
Is almost white
And waits the call to winter uses,
Garments for play and rest
And quilts to keep us warm
Through the long Alabama winter night.

Juanita Hendrix Holliman

Thanksgiving 2002

It could be a unicorn bounding across the blacktop
At barely dawn, as we head down the road toward
A Thanksgiving dinner waiting for us in Mobile.

But no unicorn, as best I can tell, only a startled doe,
In the pink November light, little more than a graceful
Shadow flitting across the Alabama highway.

Further along, pickups parked in logging roads, empty gun racks
Decorating rear windows, say that hunters are abroad
in the dark woods, crouching, guns in hands, waiting.

I think of her, lovely as a daydream, stepping lightly through
The autumn trees, her life a blur of movement in a hunter's gun
      sight,
And I wish her deliverance and sweet safety in the far woods.

Reilly Maginn

Alabama November

Discomfited nature is November's brown frown.
Her mantle of fall, a mute ginger gown.
The fairway's a sea, of soft russet waves,
Recalling the sadness of funereal graves.
Alabama now dons a frost shroud of white
Assuming the mantle of a wintry night.
Harbingers of warmth, the green roots and shoots
Will before long emerge, no one can dispute.
So don't be disheartened by ubiquitous brown
For spring's on the way. Say goodbye to brown.

Damon Marbut

the aim of pity

Late October is just the right time
in Alabama if you're in the mood to write,
if you've got a good stoop to sit on
and think under the resignation of birds.
Like you, after a hard day's work, they're looking to eat
before bed. But unlike you,
they're not granted the luxury of pulling into a store
at sunset to grab some cold beer
to take with you to feed.
They're not lucky enough to catch a neighbor
pull down her window as she's just returned
from a shower to find you staring into space,
though she thinks, or hopes, it's her naked body instead.
Nope, you'd likely tell her. Just the birds,
making snap sounds in the trees behind you,
skittering into the air
when the last chance for a meal in your yard
has failed them.
And then, some tiny frightened thing
scampers off down a branch,
and you'd like to call it a squirrel,
because it would be more familiar if it were.
But what it is is lost on you,
like the birds' idea of a snack as you, yourself,
are swarmed by mosquitoes you thought
had disappeared with the cold
as they dig into your pores,
a happy group of bellies primed to fly away
as the tiny frightened thing makes it nightly way for cover.
There's always a poem in that,
no matter who you are
getting eaten by the elements
when you think you've been excused.

Jim Reed

One of Those Thanksgiving Days in Verbena, Alabama

Field of dogs:
We're in the deep countryside, walking in their domain,
But they only welcome us
with tongues out and energetic pantings.
These are fields any childhood would find a way to enjoy.
Tall grass, fluffy dandelion wisps,
long cattails to use as gentle weapons.
No alligators in sight,
We trudge toward a drought-reduced pond
to see what was under water, hidden for so long.
The cool air matches the gray sky.
The dried and crackling weeds match the cool air and the gray sky.
We think about the century as if it holds some special quality
that previous centuries and future centuries cannot hold.
But the centuries are just made-up make-believe
centuries that change with each civilization's editing.
The crunch of dried plants under our invading soles
is the sound of the afternoon.
The rustle of leaves brushing against the lowslung belly
of an amazingly shortlegged dog is all we hear.
The giggling of children waging wars with cattails is all we hear.
No jets fly overhead,
or underfoot, for that matter.
No interstate rumblings in the distance.
Just giggles and crunchings and pitterpatter of little dog paws
and deep breaths taken down into tired citified lungs.
We walk the feast off and live at the singular moment.
The drive back to the city is a droning eventless monotone.
Home free! is what we shout when our feet touch
      our old wooden porch,
on the way to the safety of this particular century.

Julia Rowell

Blue House in Summer
Irondale, Alabama

Languid porch stretches across front
with jasmine growing and twisting
up columns wildly, and into the roof
that was one of the first to landscape
this railroad town. The mayor lived here,
they say, and his daughter who grew
to become the town's piano teacher.
She lived here unmarried until ninety.

Stepping into the life of a house,
passing ghosts of years stored silently,
shoulders brush down the halls
with crooked lines. The weight
of history slopes floors, colors
the windows blackened by a fire,
or simply the darkening of age.

Shock of Southern heat bleaches
shingles, drives bugs into the cool,
slaps you across the face
when you walk out the door.
Keeps you off the porch,
out of the vast yard,
and into the house
whose windows won't open.

Abram Ryan

To the Children of Mary of The Cathedral of Mobile

In the mystical dim of the temple
    In the dream-haunted dim of the day,
The sunlight spoke soft to the shadows,
    And said: "With my gold and your gray,
Let us meet at the shrine of the Virgin,
    And ere her fair feast pass away,
Let us weave there a mantle of glory,
    To deck the last evening of May."

The tapers were lit on the altar,
    With garlands of lilies between;
And the steps leading up to the statue
    Flashed bright with the roses' red sheen;
The sungleams came down from the heavens
    Like angels, to hallow the scene,
And they seemed to kneel down with the shadows
    That crept to the shrine of the Queen.
. . . .
And thus, in the dim of the temple,
    In the dream-haunted dim of the day,
The Angels and Children of Mary
    Met ere their Queen's Feast passed away,
Where the sungleams knelt down with the shadow
    And wove with their gold and their gray
A mantle of grace and of glory
    For the last, lovely evening of May. [2]

Vivian Smallwood

Summer Vacation
Gulf Shores, Alabama

I shall go running, running, over the yellow sand,
Hand-in-hand with the morning, toe and toe with the wind.
The pipers will run before me, keeping their distance,
And the heron, flapping his wings,
Will rise in slow retreat to the nearest dune.

All winter long I have heard the beat of the water
Over the beat of my heart, and all winter long
I have felt the surge of the wave in my surging blood.
Now April slips into May, and June will follow.
The moon-taught tide of the year will come full-flood.

Then I shall take the old road back to the sea,
Where the cabins stand on stilts, and the gulls go over,
And the lizards sleep in the sun.
I shall hear the cry of the wind and the shout of the wave,
And I shall go running, running, over the yellow sand
Where the pipers run before me and the water crowds the land.

Claiborne Schley Walsh

Fall Afternoon
Point Clear, Alabama

You don't have to be there to see it,
if you just shut your eyes and
listen quietly to yourself, you can hear the shadows,
the rumble, grunt and thunder,
the slick crack of a clean hit ball.

The leaves fell early this autumn.
Here you can smell the sweat of horse and man,
of darkened and weathered leather.
On this warm fall day, the pungent smell of
freshly mown grass litters the edges of a Point Clear field.

I am sitting on the shady side beneath the pecans
eyes shut, leaning back in a chair waiting. Listening
       for shod steel
to strike
pavement as they cross the road to begin the chukkar.

At the moment they are over in the fenced field
through the gate into the grove where
horse trailers and trucks line up
like a carney show stopped on the road.
Ponies tied to trailer sides tempt
adults and children to come pat them, feed them grass.

In the beginning, the men show neat in crisp, white breeches
and tall leather boots, colorful in their team shirts.
The horses, fresh, are sidestepping and spirited
slinging foam from tight held reins and bits.
They are not rattled, they are ready. They want to go.

In the end, the men's hair will be wet and matted, breeches
         and shirts
stained.
The last chukkar's horses will be steaming and winded.

It's a fast game, hard road to fame and not much fortune
Epithets abound among the squeak and stretch of leather,
body and horse. "I've got it!" "What the hell?" "Get the damn
thing!" Electrified, they turn and spin, rear, stop and reel
galloping downfield
toward a goalpost.

I love the game; it's pre-game, it's beginning, especially it's
         ending
where everyone relaxes, cleans and packs tack.
A camaraderie of familiarity and laughter among horses
with a few sore and very tired horsemen thrown in
         for entertainment.

Patti White

The Wind in Tuscaloosa

In the morning dusk of hurricane season,
the crape myrtle droops in a veil of rain.

Speaking of weather yet to come,

gray feathers glazed with molasses wash,
a rose stain brushed across their breasts,

a small gathering of sorrowful birds
murmurs just beneath the windowsill.

Pin-oaks drop leaves
       on the small wet lawn

as the sky spilled charcoal
       on the city streets

where, in a week of spring storms,
I watched a dove build her nest,

sparse grass on a metal fire escape,
a fragile dream laid open to the wind.

The yellow eye of the cracked egg,
gazing up from the level below,

never blinked, as the hapless dove
came day after day to check the nest,

her sad call impossibly bereft, the eye
open and hot, her cry so cool and soft.

Waiting for the eye of the storm,

I know these mourning doves are
the rain crows my mother loves

and this is what they have foretold:

my mother's voice will grow terribly thin,
a tendril of a lightless vine, a bit of dry grass

fallen from a perilous nest
        high among the breezes

that, blowing stronger,
        will steal her breath away.

Nancy Compton Williams

Thanksgiving Day in Alabama Foothills

These hills diminish
with the sun, glowing
from umber to solid
ashen gray. Only the stone
survives, baring itself
at the darkening, stark
faced, boulders holding.

They summon me across fields
to touch their boldness,
granite formed by
unforgotten fires.
Shaping my fingers to them,
I feel their flow, the molten
glowing memorized to stone.

V.

Yesterday Remembers

Joe M. Berry

Yesterday in Alabama

Four score pushes at his door
And he remembers:

The shade tree under which the men sat,
The Carrollton courthouse at their backs.
Pocketknives in their hands,
Red cedar shavings at their feet.
Straight-back, mule-eared chairs,
Caned with White Oak strips.
Checkerboards crafted from a cardboard box,
Soft drink bottle caps their checker-pieces.
Un-ironed overalls, patches patched anew,
Cotton shirts with collars turned,
Some with shoes, none with socks.
Lean with hunger,
Desperate for work.
Far-away looks in the eyes
Of Alabama men.
Looks of shame,
Looks of needing,
Looks of wanting.
It was the Great Depression years.

He remembers
When he looked through the eyes of a child
And saw a world of sadness and despair.
Remembers humor, too.

He was there that day when Great Americans were discussed.
Washington, Jefferson, Fulton, Bell, Edison,
Whitney and his cotton gin.
The latter Roosevelt was a rising star,

He offered hope,
A rare commodity under that shade tree
Of West Alabama,
The only world the little boy knew.

He was there when grown men laughed
To keep from crying.
He remembers the grown, hungry men
And their talk of their champions.
Talk of great men offered hope.
Hope for a job,
Hope for a payday,
Hope for his family eating store-bought food,
Rather than standing in the commodity line
Each Thursday for the un-bleached flour, beans, and cheese.

He remembers the talk that day,
Each man having a champion,
Each man having a king.
All their kings had fed their children,
And wore socks on their ankles.

He remembers Mr. Bridges
Sitting silently
With dime-size, wire-rimmed glasses
Hanging on the tip of his nose,
His lower lip filled with Garrett snuff.
Mr. Bridges was quiet that day,
Seemed not to have a champion,
Except his snuff.

It was serious talk that day,
Everyone looking for a king.
Hungry for food,
Hungrier still for hope.

Laughter could mask,
For a moment,
The lack of hope.

And the men needed
That moment.

The old one remembers
The champion talk running its course
And the misery of quietness
Beginning anew.
He remembers Mr. Bridges
Leaning forward in his mule-ear chair,
Spitting a mouth full of that brown
Mixture of saliva and snuff
Into the loose dirt of the courthouse lawn,
And, for a moment, allowing his
Hungry friends the luxury of laughter,
And escape of doom by saying,
"I-god boys, ole Levi Garrett weren't no damn fool."

For a moment,
The grown, hungry men laughed.
For a moment,
The laughter drowned the growling of their hungry guts.
For a moment
They had a king.

The old man remembers.

Margaret G. Cutchins

Green Promise

Little Alabama boys
want to go barefoot in March,
to feel through their soles
the throb of life in the clay.

"No sir," their mamas say,
"Not one day
before you can see new growth
on the pecan twigs."

That was black Callie's reckoning
in former times,
and what her mama had told her,
and what the mama's mama had said.

Then people paid attention
to things like that,
held a kind of pride
in family lore.

Anyway, Callie knew more
than some of the profs
over at the University
about mullein tea
for bellyaches,
tree leaf signs for planting,
leaf frost,
and little Alabama boys' bare feet. [1]

Walt Darring

Creek Days

In Alabama, where I grew up, a river
glides like a snail between its forest banks,
trailing stretches of mirrored clouds and daylight.
The water sparkles at midstream, but at its edges
it circles idly under the overhang,
where branches have fallen and leaves float in rafts,
drifting shoreward to rot in savory mulch
or off to join the flood—which still runs on,
veiling and revealing by turns its sandy bed,
wearing the green of weedy slopes and woods,
bearing commercial traffic, playing with kids
who've followed their nameless creeks down to this
historic confluence—to test themselves,
climbing and swimming with the best of them.

And then there's our creek, the familiar hole
by the railroad trestle—far from the river, but destined
to ride with it to the sea. At first it comes
babbling about rubble, rocks, and roots;
but it grows strong and silent as it wanders
through backyards in our neighborhood,
until at last it washes down to this
brown pool, just right for climbing and swimming,
with its kudzu-covered hillside, a thin path
worn by daily expeditions, the huge old oak,
the shore on our side where we sat, two boys,
nested like birds in the dense green vine . . .

If you had walked in the woods across the creek
and come upon the creekside brush that moment,
you would have seen smoke drifting downstream
or hanging like vapor over the kudzu. But who
could say where that smoke was coming from?
For we were lost to view, deep in the vine field,
smoking the vine. We called it "getting high."

One day while we were there, smoking kudzu,
the first fat drops of a rainstorm struck my head—
one, two, hard as baseballs—then a flurry of blows,
then a pelting rain—covered my head with my hands
and lit out for nowhere, having nowhere to go,
and arrived soon back at the nest in the driving rain,
with my friend beside me staring up at the clouds.
There we stood,
the cold drops running down inside our pants,
dripping from our eyelashes, filling our shoes,
there we stood, shivering but unmoved,
because there was nothing to do but prove
that we could take whatever the river dishes out,
whether that river be the destined one,
named and fixed on maps, or the other—
the one that falls from a sudden sky
like a hard freeze sent to relieve the summer heat.

James Dickey

The Escape

From my great-grandmother on,
My family lies at Fairmount
In a small rigid house of Tate marble.
A Civil War general, a small one,
Rises into the air,
Always fifty feet away,
And there are always flowers
Surrounding him as he lifts
His sword and calls back over his shoulder
To his troops, none of which lie
Under the decent plots and polished stones
Of the civilian dead. Once I saw,
Or said I did, a lily wrapped
Around his tense hand and sword hilt.
An enormous glass-fronted hospital
Rises across the street, the traffic
Roars equally from all four sides,
And often, from a textile mill,
A teen-age girl wanders by,
Her head in a singing cloth
Still humming with bobbins and looms.
In summer, the hospital orderlies eat
Their lunches on the lawn
From wet-spotted brown paper bags,
While behind them the portioned glass
Of the hospital blindingly fits
The noon sun together:
A tremendous vertical blaze
From which one piece—off-center, northwest—
Is gone, where a window is open.
I have escaped from Fairmount
Through that square hole in the light,
Having found where that piece of the sun's
Stupendous puzzle resides. It is

Lying in the woods, in a small, unfenced
County graveyard in Alabama.
It is on an open book
Of cardboard and paper, a simulated Bible,
All white, like a giant bride's,
The only real pages the ones
The book opens to; light
From the trees is falling squarely
On the few large, hand-written words.
On a hunting trip I walked through
That place, far from all relatives
And wars, from bobbins and lilies and rocks.
Because of what I had seen,
I walked through the evergreen gates
Of the forest ranger's station,
And out to my car, and drove
To the county seat, and bought
My own secret grave-plot there
For thirty-seven dollars and a half.
A young deer, a spike buck, stood
Among the graves, slowly puzzling out
The not-quite-edible words
Of the book lying under
A panel of the sun forever
Missing from the noonlight of Fairmount.
I remember that, and sleep
Easier, seeing the animal head
Nuzzling the fragment of Scripture,
Browsing, before the first blotting rain
On the fragile book
Of the new dead, on words I take care,
Even in sleep, not to read,
Hoping for Genesis. [2]

R. Garth

In Alabama

Life's best kept secret . . .
Beating in your heart's racing
Blood-red sun rays glinting off
The river (catfish musing deep in her music)
Through the open, screened, window
Of your cabin (buried deep within your nest)
Bedroom of fake, paneled wood
A/C broken (where the wasps get in)
Hot as Heaven
Sweating silver drops
Into the hellish humidity
Onto your golden breasts
A warm, wet kiss away . . .
Beer in the fridge
(Deep inside its coldness)
Fingertips clutching the ivy on my old quilt
—Grandmother went blind stitching it—
She wouldn't see this, or know
The Chickasaw word "Chewalli"—
She was from Kentucky—
But my other grandmother—
The one from here—had a
Dream deep within her soul
Of bells . . . God . . . liberty . . .
And it so seems like you, my children,
Are here . . .
*
Here, our mothers and fathers are infamous—
Each one a chiseled, clear-cut character—
Not a cut-out in the lot—
And they never, ever, leave us but in body—
But how they *lived* and *loved*—
The bloody soil is in our veins
How the sun shone in their eyes

Making love in the heat
And the river
(a train in Hank Williams cries . . .)
                      Deep . . .
                                Within Her.

John Hafner

Nostalgia

When I remember how I used to stand
Or sit or lie upon a worn-out bed
And listen to the ravings of a friend
Who never quite remembered what he read;
Or reminisce about the times we spent
On beaches where the seagulls dove for bread
While we walked past the cottages for rent
And argued about loathing, fear and dread;
Or better yet, recall the party times
At Korbett's Bar with air as light as lead
 From smoke and conversation over lines
Of poetry that we had vaguely read;
Then I regret the movements of the sun
Only a bit. But some of it was fun. [3]

Donna Holt

Fair Play

Like a bird
I pecked at Sunday dinner
begged two dollars from my daddy
hurried out the door

stepped into Debbie's shiny red GTO, rushed to Athens
raced up and down North Jefferson
burned rubber from Hardee's to Burger Chef—
Bibles lying in the back seat.

Stole kisses from football-player boyfriends
at an old abandoned church near Lucy's Branch
smoked a little reefer planned our futures—
got back to church in the nick of time.

My daughter begged me for five dollars today
nibbled at her dinner ran outside and got
into Mary's blue Toyota.

I curl on the couch like a helpless kitten.
I regret having thought my mama stupid.

Yvonne Kalen

Wake Up, America

Whether I travel north, east, or west,
the minute I open my mouth and speak,
I'm greeted with "Oh, you're from the South.
I just love to hear you people talk."
I want to say "we people are your people,"
But I'm polite and say "how kind."

You can see the wheels grind—the thought
Southerners may not be exceptionally bright.
Let me say, "The banjo is no longer on our knees,
and brains abound in our heads.

In Alabama, we understand fast talk,
but we're in no hurry. We drawl.
This leaves no time for boring chatter."

The question then sarcastically posed is:
"Did you feel the hurricane in Alabama?"

"Oh yes, a little rain and wind to clean things up,
but we can handle it in Alabama . . ."

By the way, you will probably be surprised
to hear we have fine universities,
complete with well-known professors.
We have a fair amount of doctors, lawyers,
and some good old boys.

Wake up, America . . .
Alabama is part of the U.S.A.

Marjorie Lees Linn

Outside the Shadows

> ... they live in a steady shame and insult of discomforts, insecurities, and inferiorities, piecing these together into whatever semblance of comfortable living they can, and the whole of it is a stark nakedness of makeshifts and a lack of means.
>
> —James Agee, *Let Us Now Praise Famous Men*

Part of the whole of it,
whose feet knew floors
of Alabama clay
worn smooth and hard as slate,
whose eyes reflected light
diffused through windowpanes
of paper
greased in rendered fat
to brown translucency:
brief heir to shame and insult,
whose life held nakedness
as lightly as a dream.
Never quite believing either one.
More sure of silence
and the promises of silence.

My life holds yesterday
more lightly than a dream.

*My feet touched marble
stained with amber light!*

I stand
outside the shadows of the makeshift
and the lack.
The silence
blooms.
We sing. [4]

Susan Martinello

Night Train

Alabama night train croons,
sidetracks sleep, rumbles and wails
me down the remembering rails.

Sensations crawl like evening shadows
across the ceiling of a sick room,
gather like dew drops on a toddler's feet.

A child's trust in her world of rose-sprigged linens
rises like boiled milk, subsides, holds
like the permanent waves of childless women

who shared cinnamon sugar toast
and cookies with a brown-eyed little girl.
People come strong—people who loved me long,

and grandparents whose love drifted out
on the miles: transcontinental train song.
Places course the underpasses of dream—

garden of stone-cold table and tree roots like steps,
library coupling paper-scent and story-crossings,
wharf where high-tossed cones took wing,

ice cream still melting on land-bound tongues:
this midnight zoetrope of the senses.
When train call fades like an afternoon

of grass blades on skin, my ears yearn
for the persistent summons of the sweet-talking train,
the distant rolling rumble

of car after car of dark-bound lading
throwing phantoms like sparks off the tracks,
a kind of listening for the final run.

Shelia Smith Mau

Dried Apples and Cotton Ticking

The old screened door framed June's moonlight,
on a night soft with cricket sounds.
Pale rays wound back to me,
on the small cot in the dogtrot hall.

Apples, apples smelled everywhere,
dried and fused to my soul.
Made my mind's eye recall
Grandmother and last fall's apples
sliced like small crescent moons
browning slowly in the sun.

She would spread them first outside to dry
on a quilt under hot Alabama sky.
But when night and all its coolness fell
and shoved Indian summer and Granny's apples in,
she would put them there—
on top of the cot in the dogtrot hall.
Apples, apples to my bed!

Now, in memories of seasons there,
my dreams still smell
of dried apples and cotton ticking.

Samuel Minturn Peck

The Grapevine Swing

When I was a boy on the old plantation
Down by the deep bayou,
The fairest spot of all creation,
Under the arching blue;
When the wind came over the cotton and corn
To the long slim loop I'd spring
With brown feet bare, and a hat brim torn,
And swing in the grapevine swing.

Swinging in the grapevine swing,
Laughing where the wild birds sing,
I dream and sigh
For the days gone by
Swinging in the grapevine swing.

Out o'er the water lilies bonnie and bright,
Back to the moss-grown trees;
I shouted and laughed with a heart as light
As a wild rose tossed by the breeze.
The mocking bird joined in my reckless glee,
I longed for no angel's wing,
I was just as near heaven as I wanted to be
Swinging in the grapevine swing.

Swinging in the grapevine swing,
Laughing where the wild birds sing.
Oh, to be a boy
With a heart full of joy,
Swinging in the grapevine swing.

I'm weary at noon, I'm weary at night,
I'm fretted and sore of heart,
And care is sowing my locks with white
As I wend through the fevered mart.
I'm tired of the world with its pride and pomp,
And fame seems a worthless thing.
I'd barter it all for one day's romp,
And a swing in the grapevine swing.

Swinging in the grapevine swing,
Laughing where the wild birds sing,
I would I were away
From the world today,
Swinging in the grapevine swing.

Lora Perry

Alabama Treasure

I see beneath a caption the image
of your round, young face,
first Lora, love of Clarke County.
I gaze and wish aloud your wreath of hair
had been my legacy. My audience replies,
"The bouffant covers pads."
I alter my wish
and covet your skill.

Your eyes speak melancholy,
a humor you bequeathed to me
with frequent warning
to abandon gloom
and think in brisk allegro.

The lace yoke rising high
to cover your neck
shows modesty applauded
in that day and still with you
when you admonished,
"Young ladies should not parade
around town in shorts."

Your virtue I admire.
Yet I must chide you
for directing modesty awry.
Years passed before you left us,
time enough for you to tell
what none of us would know
until your grandson,
digging among archival roots,
unearthed a dusty treasure:
"Beautiful Women of Alabama"
The Montgomery Advertiser, May 3, 1908.

Kathleen Petersen

Reminiscences of Mid-Century Alabama

Sun kissed, we walked down grassy alleys
lined with tangled blackberry bushes,
fruit so sweet we ate it off the vine—
laughing as the juice, warm and purple,
ran down our chins staining the soft cotton
of halter tops that matched our shorts—
everything matched in those days.
Long summer drives ended in picnics,
a simple feast enjoyed beside a river,
its water warm against our skin
when finally mama let us jump in.
We spent hours at the movies—
the only place that had air conditioning—
shrieking at scary films as girls will do,
laughing at funny ones,
dreamily living the love stories,
enjoying cool air against our sunburned skin.
On Sundays, after church and fried chicken,
we lazed the day away in reading.
A quarter bought us a bag of candy
and a popsicle, red, blue or green.
It all tasted much better way back then,
when we lived, slow and sweet,
and, sun kissed, began to walk down the years.

Bonnie Roberts

Poems of Mine Readers Cannot Follow

I cannot follow, either,
and I am the one who wrote the doors.

When I touch the knobs or latches,
they burn or freeze my hands.
And sometimes the wood,
a thousand-told tale,
falls into dust at my feet,
and behind the doors, blank walls.

Some nights, I do find a secret hall
that leads to the voice of my father.
He is playing an LP of Nat King Cole,
but he says,
"Sugar, this record is worn out."
He points to the warm warps and scratches.
"We need a new record,
but this one is not made anymore."

He points down the hall to the room of blood,
but we don't go there.
Our feet are frozen.
We know what is there,
and Daddy says, "I've been shocked to forget that,"
and I say, "The shock has made me remember
my whole life."

We turn around, pushing through doors
the thickness of steel vaults,
but our loyal dog, Tongue, is waiting
on the other side by Wilson Lake
with a stick for us to throw.
I say, "Daddy, Tongue is dead."
He says, "That's okay, darlin'. I'm dead, too."

And all the doors fall away,
and I am left at a **No Entrance** sign
on some street in Florence, Alabama,
in front of the disused Shoals Theater--
its marquee boasting only a lopsided red "L"—
near the post office and the park with the goldfish pond
where someone has thrown in a silver gum wrapper
and horns are blowing.
I am holding up traffic that is going somewhere.
I am not able to follow myself home.
And no one could follow me there.
The pines on the hill on Cloverdale Road
have all been cut down,
along with the tire swing,
the white rag tied on
where Tongue grabbed on by his teeth
and swung out with us.

And Daddy, after the tragedy, walks the floor
just like he always did,
until early morning,
working out mathematical theorems
to block out the scratchy music,
or reading *The Red and the Black*
at the dining room table,
muttering to himself in foreign languages.
And Tongue, who disappeared
after the shot rang out,
has never been seen again,
except when I try to bring my readers here.
Maybe he hides behind a door,
whimpering for my sister,
or just for someone to mend
the screen he tore through
that night
to escape

to where I cannot follow.

Charles Rodning

Sense of Place: Sweet Home Alabama

wagon wheel
beside an old shed—
rollin' nowhere

***

walkin'
a road shrouded in fog
home

***

drippin' sweat . . .
waitin' . . . for the water pump
. . . to turn cold

***

cut hay
along a red clay road
heavy on the breeze

***

cornstalks
rustling
darkness

***

twilight shadows
slower than a dragonfly
on a weathered dock

***

one raindrop—
all the colors
of the sun

***

deep river
flowing quietly
to the sea

***

harvest moon
rising over
slow thunder

***

off to school—
grandma' wavin' from
her kitchen window

***

grandma's rockin' chair
hidden in tall thick grass
sittin' . . . empty . . .

***

rumpled teapot
beside grandma's shed—
whistlin' with the wind

***

mama's apple crate—
overflowing with
marigolds

***

mama's rhubarb pie
coolin' on the window sill—
"think we can reach it?"

***

dusty pasture—
playin' hide-and-seek
in the junk cars

***

"cotton-candy" kiss—
ridin' a ferris wheel
above a harvest moon

***

night light—
porch swing
screechin' . . . empty

***

following
a path of moonlight
thru a pathless woods

Joseph Sackett

Ghosts

They come unannounced,
Quietly, almost imperceptive,
Like pale whispers on a delicate wind.
Some say they don't exist,
But I know better.
Others do too.
In places like this,
Old Mobile,
With its damp, clammy clime,
Where every little summertime nit reaches out
To climb, slip, crawl upon your skin,
How can one not believe?

They wander about,
Quite leisurely, it seems,
With no particular reason
As to who is here and who is not.
Most come and go as they please.
Tragedy plays well in their world,
But many are lighthearted, playful too.
Some are devilishly mischievous,
Others with no more malice
Than a humble field mouse.

Do they choose who discern them?
Perchance.
That might explain why some
Sense their presence
While others cannot.
Perhaps a key is given,
All cloak-and-dagger, mind you,
To a providential few,
That they may unlock, unravel
Mysteries of a rare family tree—

A tree whose roots often struggle
To rise above the ground.
If so, I consider myself blessed
To be a keeper of such a key.
For I can surely feel their presence
On dark, restless summer nights,
When this old town's damp air
Rolls sultry down my cheek,
All steamy and dreamy
In its own muggy way.
And that's fine by me.
I'm not troubled, as you can see.
In fact, I rather enjoy their company. [5]

Sonia Sanchez

Present

This woman vomiting her
hunger over the world
this melancholy woman forgotten
before memory came
this yellow movement bursting forth like
coltrane's melodies all mouth
buttocks moving like palm trees,
this honeycoatedalabamianwoman
raining rhythm of blue / black / smiles
this yellow woman carrying beneath her breasts
pleasures without tongues
this woman whose body weaves
desert patterns,
this woman, wet with wandering,
reviving the beauty of forests and winds
is telling you secrets
gather up your odors and listen
as she sings the mold from memory.

      there is no place
for a soft / black /woman.
there is no smile green enough or
summertime words warm enough to allow my growth.
and in my head
i see my history
standing like a shy child
and i chant lullabies
as i ride my past on horseback
tasting the thirst of yesterday tribes
hearing the ancient / black / woman
me, singing   hay-hay-hay-hay--ya-ya-ya.
                        hay-hay-hay-hay-ya-ha-ya.
like a slow scent
beneath the sun

                        and i dance my
creation and my grandmothers gathering
from my bones like great wooden birds
spread their wings
while their long / legged / laughter
stretches the night.
                    and i taste the
seasons of my birth. mangoes. papayas.
drink my woman / coconut / milks
stalk the ancient grandfathers
sipping on proud afternoons
walk with a song round my waist
tremble like a new / born / child troubled
with new breaths
                and my singing
becomes the only sound of a
blue / black / magical / woman. walking.
womb ripe. walking. loud with mornings. walking.
making pilgrimage to herself. walking.

Teresa K. Thorne

Alabama Dreams in Black and White

Azalea smiles and honeysuckle voices
'bless a heart' with careful knives.
To porch-rocker rhythm and blues
grey-bearded oaks and trailer geezers
remember younger days dusted in red clay—
fields of dreams,
and dreams of glory,
power makers, power shakers,
chink of ice in sweet topaz tea,
once a sound of bourbon on the rocks—
gentle men opening doors.
Closed doors.
Freedom fighters murmuring discontent,
through sticky summers
beneath the purr of ceiling fans,
mourning war days' glory.
Slow, stirring . . . shaking, waking from the dream,
meandering through the kudzu tangle
of politics and deals
and firefly nights.

Frank X Walker

Fireproof
after the burning of a church in the black belt

the heart
of the bible belt
is steepled
the souls of church folk
have pews
the home of gospel music
has been forever altered
because only a devil
could set fire
to a church

but church people
are like fire ants
as soon as the smoke clears
they'll be stirring up cement
testing new extinguishers
installing a smoke alarm
in the pulpit

before you can say
revelations
chapter twenty
verses seven through ten
they will stop moaning and wailing
and sift through the ashes

tip over charred and smoky stained glass
looking for the mourners' bench
and come Sunday
twice as many worshippers
will pray on it
from across
the street

under a tree
counting pennies
and their blessings
starting a new building fund
'til the roof is raised
and the foundation poured
again
thanking the Lord
for a new day
and their right minds
regretful for needing
such a powerful message
to continue believing
that God is good and wise and merciful
offering up prayers
for them that done the deed
asking the Lord
to touch their dark hearts
smother out all that evil
guide them
on a straighter narrower path
forever
forgiving

church people
are fireproof
and Faith
won't just go up
in smoke

Jamie Yerby

**when we come home
or
moving miles away from nothing**

we're leaving soon,
this dirty red road,
limbs left from ivan,
like alligators that stalk
the driveway;

we're leaving
the green country miles,
  and miles,
     and miles,
for saner land
with grocery stores
and garbage pickup;

we're leaving
the serpents that hide
in untrimmed Alabama grass,
edging a once pristine lake
barely noticed now,
even with six feet windows
that watch like eyes
the crane or geese
with their young;

we're leaving
the yellowed green fields
off dusty two lane roads,
where stoic cows
wait patiently in a pasture
for the day when the trucks come;

we're leaving
the camouflage,
the random guns shots at night,
the manic chihuahua next door
with her incessant bark at dawn;

we're leaving my lilies
over grown with ivy,
and a lawn where dandelions kill roses,
and neighbors burn garbage;

we're leaving
the sunset,
the still presence of autumn leaves
playing narcissus in the lake,
the fireflies that swarm light
like nighttime county stars;

. we'll miss them,
but we'll plant our own happiness
along the front of our blue house;

i'll get gardenias to grow
in dark earth,
and hydrangeas to bloom
their pastel orbs;
i'll sit in our fenced yard
with my dogs
and enjoy them again;
i'll string hammocks in the shade
on days when we want to get away,
without driving twenty miles;

we'll live again
in civilized country,
where dental care
surrounds our neighborhood,
and azalea blooms we'll watch,
with anticipation

not like the country
where we rush by,
ignorant of pink blossoms,
or simply forget them,
just as we will
the country

when we come home.

VI.

Nature Remembers

Steve Bailey

An Alabama Night Walk:
June 1983

Out for a walk into the night.
The sky is dark,
but for the stars so bright
with their moonless light.

A grove of trees in the distance
stands like a backdrop:
solid, all of the same scene—
a feature of eternity.

Fireflies dance through the trees,
twinkling wonders of nature.
They echo each other's entry,
joined together by destiny.

I watch the piece with mesmerized eyes;
a revelation it seems,
made soul-breakingly clear that the fireflies
seem with the sky—

with the sky to be one,
       one with the stars,
              one with me
                     and Destiny.

Robin Behn

Patton Lake, Tuscaloosa

for my son at two

The mud flats stink like sun-cracked haunches of dead horses.
How long it takes to die, which battle, they won't say.

We count survivors: Conestoga mailbox, inlet jammed
        with turtles,
swarms of invading three-pointed kudzu stars.

First I'm diving uphill, flat-out, pushing the stroller,
one hand down on your cheek, the awning yawning

green unto collapse above our heads,
then it's time for you to put your full-grown hand

to my cheek at the end or a little before the end.
Whatever's in between

will someday be dead horses who won't know
they were petted or that, tonight, the moon

almost came all the way down in, or into,
this our life. It's time to go.

But you say, once more, *roundaroundaround!*
For this is the hour of flowers

furling up petals, of kudzu's groggy rocking
in the hard-soft hammock of its *u*'s.

Hour when the ducklings—recently, utterly, disappeared—
might shine up through the murk—

If ever all the animals are gone from you,
the farm set bare and the word you need to name

the stall door's rattle
—house- or thimble-sized, hay-scarred, horrible—

is one I took with me
or one I never said,

remember golden ducklings
could be coins in a fountain,

or lovely yellow streetlights under a turtle sky,
or the *Red-Blue-Yellow-Shoe* yellow

of the yellow thing the first time you said *yellow*—
Anything is beautiful

or anything is something else
and that thing, then, is beautiful

or something that is something that is
something that is beautiful.

Bury the language with me
that kept me, afternoons, from you.

Take what's left around.
Sing what's left: a round.

Patricia Crosby Burchfield

Freedom of the River

The river steals into the scenery it traverses without intrusion, silently creating and adorning it, and is as free to come and go as the zephyr.
— Henry David Thoreau

Among the reeds the river flows,
Bending in a graceful arc,
Carrying leaves and twigs
Downstream in swirling
Eddies of dark water;
Flowing underneath the bridge, past
Gnarled Cypress trees, and shallow
Habitat of darting fish,
Into unplumbed depths of Devil's Hole.
Jumping mullet splash three times,
Knifing through the summer air
Like programmed robotic fish.
Magnolia River's own aquatic show.
Nine solemn turtles ride a drifting
Oak limb down the river, while
Pelicans in formation fly over the
Quicksilver water and a gently
Rocking wooden fishing boat.
Sunning Cottonmouth Moccasin
Twists his way through thick
Undergrowth at the water's edge;
Venus fly-trap, Pitcher plants,
Waterlillies with broad pads, and
Xanthic Black-eyed Susans
Yield to the wake of a silver boat
Zipping southward toward Mobile Bay.

Happy days, free days, and Joy to you.
Pat Burchfield
*200_*

Bettye Kramer Cannizzo

Dance of the Yellowhammers

Like stately sandhill cranes,
the flickers are elegant
in their courtship ritual.

Black-bibbed breasts
trapping sunlight:

Gray-capped heads,
scarlet napes,
tilt skyward:

necks stretching,
bills waving.

Crescendoes crashing,
yellow underwings flashing.

Flowing with flair
like Rogers and Astaire,
the yellowhammers dance. [1]

Carol Case

Wildlife Sanctuary

I sit on a dead tree stump
in a bog north of Mobile, Alabama
almost every Sunday morning
as my brothers and their wives sit
beside strangers at First Baptist.
They sing and smell of aftershave
while I search for signs and wonders.

Here pitcher plants lift leaves
like arms raised in prayer
above the ankle-deep waterline.
Their mouths gape open and pause
hold the last note of a hymn,
and wait for the organist
to move her feet from the pedals.

The guidebook explains how
a bog must burn to survive,
to die out and be born again,
in a ritual ancient as the moon.
Charred pine trunks stand witness,
a testament to the purifying flames.

I pronounce the botanical names,
match the leaf in my hand
with the picture in the book
as my nephews in Sunday clothes
prop their chins for the litany of begatting
and gaze out the window
across fields to where the bog begins.

Mary Brobston Cleverdon

Nesting

We drove with Verda to the River Styx
to look at egrets in their nesting place.
The road ran straight past plotted farms, then wove
around the scrubby hills, dense undergrowth,
descended to the creeks, along the swamp
that offered a dim prospect of our watch.

Verda, the expert eyes on the bird watch,
pointed out the nests, untidy stacks of sticks,
each tended by the parents in the swamp –
one on the nest, one swooping to the place,
bug bristling in its beak, urging to growth
a set of mouths. The other sat and wove

A magic by its constancy. They wove
a life out there, bound by their watch—
turning a fresh crew of feathery growths
into a flock of fliers, to leave the Styx
and span the green fields of a different place,
miles and miles from the rookery swamp.

All who can, of course, come back to the swamp
as time unravels the pattern woven
in the brain, or sinews, or whatever place
instinct sits coils like the springs of a watch.
I return by memory, by what sticks
in my mind, witnessing that scene of growth.

The children with us then are now grown-up.
They called it a 'bird factory,' the swamp,
and laughed with Verda clucking on about those sticks,
wishing the egrets would learn to weave
neater nests, keep a better watch-out
for the turkey buzzards circling the place.

Couldn't the parents see them settling into place
at the tops of dead trees, above the lush growth,
the vines and palmetto thickets, watching
for a chick to topple out, feathers swamped—
see them sitting there, poised to weave
their way downward to dinner on the Styx?

Observers all, we grew used to the dark swamp,
even to the hawk-eyed figures, woven in place,
keeping the stillest watch on the River Styx. [2]

A. M. Davis

This Alabama Earth

This earth once buried a swath of secret sins
before its hardening, its congelation into concrete,
before it turned itself into an extension of the gravel above
and yielded nothing but an indiscriminate horizon
on the backs of the un-beautiful,
while lonely growths stemmed between the cracks in sidewalk
without blossoming their ends.

It admonishes itself for hating its children,
as if it had been waiting for a family who didn't deserve
dirt embedded in the lines along their knuckles.
It had become disgusted with those ruddy knees,
those popping joints or jaw bones.

Once, it wore its reddest dress for cotton kings,
clayed its ankles
in affairs with the fathers of progress.

Once, it rouged an awful smile, then bloodied
its own lip with shame
so the lovers of iniquity would fight to hold its hand,
so the church would see its welt and wound
and have to still be sorry.

It danced with sons of slaves, of princes.
It told exquisite stories, this earth.
Under its petticoat, no unwelcome fingers found their pleasure.
Behind the fan, no demurity or smile.
What it wanted in the beginning, it still aches for in the end:
the recognition of someone important or sincere.

Yes, it waits,
its pelvis bruised in black and white.
When it holds itself in front of mirrors,
its image blurs by the smudge and uncertainty of its choices.
It buries them, then itself,
with a glance over its shoulder like a whore
who has so much more to hide.

Dwight Eddins

The Tombigbee at Naheola

Married to water, fused with rock,
these names eluded the ethnic cleansing.
And now they float in the owl's derision,
the scorn of the hawk inviolate
above the morbid ebb of empire:
timber for Nagasaki, coal
to stoke the Rising Sun's ascension.
Down a river gutted by engineers,
slow barges are bearing the picked
black bones of the gutted land.
From the high bluff's derelict heaven
the discontinued gods keep watch,
chalk masks of apprehension.
There are no words for this at the closed
P.O.: no spells to stem this tide,
no holy names to exorcise
the dark approach of the coffin makers. [3]

Charles Ghigna

The Alabama Elm

The elms here are easy to talk about,
though we never really take them one at a time,
never really know one with words.

Maybe our eyes are the problem,
and when we close, our hands, too,
get in the way.

We almost cannot walk by an elm
with our fingers still in our pockets,
and I wonder if it is their silence

that we want each time to touch
or simply the feel of something stronger
than ourselves, something rooted and solid

that may tell the truth on us
whenever we come out of our pockets
and open our eyes. [4]

Juliana Gray

Peaches

In 1967, my father brought
my mother to his home in Chilton County.
She asked, flirtatiously, "I thought they were
supposed to grow a lot of peaches here.
Where are they? All I see is pine and clay."
He drove her through the country roads for hours,
past every orchard, until she cried "enough."
Then he showed the plant where he had worked
his teenage summers, picking and sorting fruit
so hot that some collapsed to overripe
nectar in his hands.

                    He told me this
some thirty-five years later as we toured
a packing plant in Georgia. On catwalks, we strolled
above the migrant workers, who boldly stared
at us without pausing from their work.
We spooned peach ice cream in our frozen mouths.
As he talked, my father's voice was edged
with envy for machinery, the sprays
and belts and sorting trays he hadn't had
the chance to use when he had done this job.

I had forgotten peaches until a friend
shared an August basketful with me.
We tore them open with our teeth, sucked
the juice between our fingers, pulled the meat
from clinging blood-red stones and ate it raw.
It tasted good. That's all. We ate the fruit,
and wiped our mouths, and did not think of more.

Theodore Haddin

How Trees Go Down in Alabama

For Thomas Brown, December 1998

We look toward the hill where there was
no light and we find them after fall
when leaves are gone
and they the ones went down in leaf
a lightning stripe still cast in bark
and mold already white and cold and damp
or the long-standing pine attacked
by beetles has finally fallen
from years of weight it can no longer hold
or some woodsman has tested his strength
against a harmless temptation but missed
and pushed a tree upon a fence
and then there are those we find
after storms wrecks of oaks and poplars
twisted and thrown up by gusts and the tornado
that just missed the house
like the neighbor's thoughtless clear-cut
I saw a wind one day turn
a whole hillside to splinters
a strange light in a wild storm
and one winter I heard ice in forms
snap a hundred trees all night
till none were left but broken trunks
and treetops clogged the still streams

B. Kim Hagar

Night Reverie on Elk River
for my Mom

We sit out back
on the dock
watch the Elk River
run backwards in
the moonlight
wishing for just one
breath of breeze
in this flannel air.
Memories come easy here—
and I think of Mama's stories
of picking cotton
and how they would come in
from the fields
at lunch time
lie in the floor
the linoleum cooling their
hot skin—
almost too hot to eat
until time to go back.

The Elk River peels away time
like thin onion skin.
I imagine Mama
8 years old,
blinding blond hair,
and Lillie Mae,
with warm latte skin
towering over her
from the next row, saying
"Now come on, Betty.
I'll catch you up to my row"—
Mama couldn't keep up.

Lillie Mae would lift her voice
in song
pick up the pace
so they could finish and go home . . .

You can smell cotton
in a field on a
hot Alabama day—
a scent like no other,
something you would know forever
once you've smelled it,
like drawing near the Elk River—
something unique, a scent of life.

Days when Granddaddy was
off to the gin with a wagon,
my Grandmother tallied
cotton sack weights at the
end of the day
on a piece of cardboard
tacked onto the other wagon,
like scores from some odd game
while Mama would jump and play
in the wagon—
the mounds like soft, hot snow—
helping to pack down the cotton.

The Elk River runs backwards
sometimes . . .
thanks to TVA.
We sit out back on the dock,
tell old stories,
reminisce,
calling back days of cotton
our children will never know.

Dennis Hale

Elba Beware!

Snaking across southeast
Alabama, Pea River
slithers around Elba,
eager to strike again,
lacking only the heavy foot
of limitless rain
on her sensitive skin.
Elba, beware!
the serpentine menace
vipertines on the edge
of your manicured garden,
your original sin.
Elba, beware!
tempted to build
fences against the tide,
you cannot.
you lie
defenseless,
Eden beneath
the coils of a restless scourge.
Pea River will rise
again and hiss,
and piss on Elba,
poor Elba,
Elba beware! [5]

Jerri Hardesty

Night Does Not Fall

In Alabama,
Night does not fall, it rises;
Rises from the catfish depths
Of dark running Dixie rivers,

Rises from the crouching shadows
Hidden beneath Southern Pines
Waiting for their proper time,

Rises from asphalt-black city streets
Flowing with Southside jazz
And urban rhythms,

Rises from the quicksilver surfaces
Of oakbound lakes,
Cool and full of bass promises,

Rises from the soft-loam earth,
Smelling of spices, sustenance,
And the toil of hands,

Rises from the iron ore mountains,
Their tanned, brawny backs
Turned on sultry setting sun,

Rises from wildflower-sweet meadows
With song of whippoorwill, blink of firefly,
And scent of honeysuckle,

Rises from the salt-swirled waves,
Devouring crystalline beaches
In hightide buffets,

Rises from the shady sides of downtown silhouettes
Stretching daylight's last reflection,
Snapping back neon replies,

Rises from the whisper of skirts,
Swaying on hips, lush with humidity
And feminine grace,

Rises from the somber clouds of a stormy past,
Electric with the enlightened hope of a brighter future,
Sleeping in far dreaming hearts and minds,

And I rise to meet it!
    Don't you?

Kennette Harrison

Alabama Afterstorm

Next twilight
after the thunderous
night of lightning
after the searing of sky
after the singeing of air
after the loud announcements
of doom thunder-clapped themselves
into our collective hearts

after children piled into bed
with parents pretending bravery
after fierce dogs quaked
with knowledge
of cracked-open heavens
and slunk back
from watchdogging

next twilight
we were alive again
and our faces put away
their frowns and tears
we were steady in ourselves
and we welcomed the ordinary
saw its detail, and no one
was discontent

but after the terrible
that next twilight
things were still not
perfectly right
not until
the magic

after sunset
in the pause
before night

when electric earth
which wars with heaven
which feeds us and then
receives at last
our mortal selves
when this darkening earth
broke into gift enough
for all.

Children stopped in wonder
as some invisible
secret signal
turned on in Alabama
and there arose
from June grass
living lights
blinking miracle
miracle.

Children chased little stars
come to earth, and shouted
"Lightnin' bugs, lightnin' bugs"
and parents kissed sons
and daughters, and forgot
the storm's terrors.
Grandparents rocked
and watched, and loved
the twinkling earth
embraced it, as it would
soon embrace their very
mortal selves.

Ava Leavell Haymon

Coelenterata: Gulf Shores, Alabama

The early morning sea is brown,
the shore littered with stranded jellyfish.
My eyes are swollen from yesterday's salty swim,
the margaritas, a smoky Holiday Inn pillow.
One scrap of last night's dream bobs free,
summoned by the festering ocean:
    my own head, sundered
        from its neck.

The water is full of these things!
a whine, our first words of the morning.
We've carried coffee to the beach, in styrofoam,
to wake up easy by a tourist ocean. But before
it tips, each breaker thins to show us
red-tentacled tissue against the trough behind—
    ugly clots, slack, without will, pulsed
        only by the single-minded surf.

No brain, my factual daughter recalls:
No skeleton. 99% water. They are nothing but sacks.
And then an adolescent gearshift from scientist
to theologian: *So how do they die?* The viscous blobs
evaporate to nothing as the sand heats up.
How do they live? my only answer at middle-age.
My bloated dream unsnags its drowned moorings,
buoys toward me out of sleep:
    severed head, eyes open,
        passed from hand to hand.

Jay Higginbotham

Bitchina

Over the sands of Isle Dauphine,
On past the Eastern Shore,
Bitchina comes a-howling,
wreaking grief and gore.

Across the swells of Mobile Bay,
Past the red clay hills,
Bitchina swamps the Causeway row,
engulfing all its frills.

Thus through the night Bitchina yowls,
And shrieks and bares her wrath.
She shatters water oaks and pines
And roofs as with a snath.

"But what did we to rate such woe?"
I beg Bitchina tell:
"Have you no shame or pity
Than to loose the hounds of hell?"

"O ye of little ken," she cries.
"Can not you grasp the hue?
For demons yet more menacing
I am preparing you."

"As, in my wake, a different storm,
Far more fierce than I,
Will strike to test the worthiness
Of all you glorify."

"So curse me not," Bitchina squalls.
"I'm no mere wild coquette,
But Madre Nature's Ariel—
Awake to what you've met!"

Evelyn Hurley

To Alabama

I love the roar of wild March tantrums,
snowy surprises, premature blooms,

the taste of April in the mountains,
dogwood petals bleeding scars,

the orange and yellow days of summer,
riverbeds dimpled with pearls of polished stones,

fields glowing in October's amber light,
pastures rolled with rounds of pungent hay,

frost that kisses tight persimmon flesh
and brings her ripe to glory—orange and brown.

I love days when the broom sage sways and smiles,
when singing wind redeems the earth with seed,

sunrise and the fading of the light,
as winter folds us safely into rest,

the quilted sleep of Alabama nights,
benedictions softly falling in the rain.

Mary Brunini McArdle

Alabama Sunset

I lived well west of here before.
It never had occurred to me
That daylight ended sooner
In my new-found home.
My biorhythms still
Have not adjusted to the loss
Of thirty minutes.

The sun doesn't set
In North Alabama—not exactly;
The prelude is like any other sunset:
A brilliant yellow circle
Sinking slowly toward
The accepting rim of Earth,
The colors of the sky
Changing as the afternoon
Comes to an end.

And then—suddenly—
Before there is a chance
For said circle
To grow ponderous and darken,
It drops—like a beach ball
Lost from a toddler angel
Messing in God's toybox.

Tom McDougle

A Blue-Tailed Lizard on the Porch of Alabama's Oldest Wood-Framed House
Mooresville, Late Summer, 1992

Slipping up between oak floor boards his head
    appears like a thumb through thick cracked fingers.
He is the color of stone, gray except
    for its iridescent satin tail blue.
Blue as the eyes of Neptune; ocean blue.

The tail is an evolutionary
    mask. The mask is an appearance that dis-
    closes reality beyond appearance.
Like other masks, it bespeaks protection.
It bespeaks a smooth ether of sacred
    mystery. [6]

Jessica McNealy Miles

Seven Ways to Look at Tiny Minnows

Time moves back, slows down in this season
sizzled with the motions of river waters now fat and silver,
fed plump as children's cheeks, by April-shower clouds.
Spring is when Earth wears her burden-blessing to continue
the only time of year to play at the edges
of all the loves we almost can't remember.

Tiny minnows like old men who try to remember
the how and when of what it was like, season
the licks and laps of a pond's edge.
My child-self often employed in trapping those silver
slipping bodies. My hand punctured continuously
into their cold, azure, fluid cloud.

Too many cotton-ball-clouds
drift through my Alabama past to remember,
but the feeling of them over head as they continue
by shading in waves the first flowers of the season,
will always be part of how I see silver
lace around puffy white edges.

Spring is a new kind of edge—
singular, repeated. Like the dispositions of a cloud,
or the thirty-seven-thousand shades of a tiny minnow's silver.
Spring is always and never the same as human minds remember.
More than just a season
it is the blood and bones, cells and sinews of continuation.

But, spring does not bear the consequences one faces
       when continued.
It does not bring with it the sharp edge
and the forceful blade of other seasons,
that must carry with them the clouds
left over, unrained down. Winter clouds remember
the shiver unused in seedtime, like unspent silver.

Winter, as beautiful as it seems, with snow-silver
hillsides and crystal-crisp air continues
to chant in bird's ears, "remember
you are not home here in this water's edge,
somewhere South, there is a warmer, whiter cloud,
and a much nicer greener season."

So this season creeps, away from such snow-silver,
and to a warmer whiter cloud. And we, left back, continue
to tip-toe down the edge of youth, loaded with slippery things
       to remember.

Barry Marks

Shelby County Coyote

or maybe a fox, he had no place
in the woods between our deck and
our neighbor's new swimming pool,
but there he was, trotting off toward I-65
like he was surveying his own backyard,
not 20 miles from the Jefferson County Courthouse.

What if he is the advance scout
for a war party, the dispossessed
risen to reclaim their birthright?
He will return with others of his kind
and bear, boar, bison
bent on driving us back to Birmingham.

They will attack just before dawn,
led, no doubt, by a reconnaissance squad
of bats squeaking the coordinates.
The attackers will set up perimeters
(squirrels should make superb sentries)
and a mobile HQ atop the water tower.
A gaggle of geese will provide air cover,
sacrificing themselves into F-16 intakes and
Apache blades when the National Guard counterattacks.

Perhaps they will enlist allies
among the insect world: roaches, flies
and spiders putting off their internecine conflict
to unite against the poisoning, heavy-footed foe;
or worse, they will send emissaries
to the ghost-shirted assassins,
microbes, bacilli and fungi,
the mutating viral horde,
to sweep off their reservations
and attack with lethal bio-weaponry.

Olde Weatherly will fall to the insurrectionists,
then New Weatherly and the nameless
office park across the street.
They will reclaim 665 Weatherly Lane.
Vines will violate our precious possessions,
choking Beanie Babies and Barbies,
evicting Monet prints from our walls.
A family of armadillos will nest in the master bath,
while deer doze in our bed and a solitary opossum
sways in my hammock.

The occupying force
will forage the pantry, Shermanizing,
animal bummers loaded down
with Fritos and Fruit Roll-ups
scurrying into the wild night.

They will eat my daughter's loyalist dog;
I assume the cats
will quickly turn coat.

As a final indignity, some furry lockpick
will free our parakeets
to soar out the shattered bay window
into the spring air, their wings
stretched in unfettered glory,
celebrating the joy
of the undomesticated sun.

Carter Martin

Visiting Waterfalls in Bankhead Forest

At Kinlock Falls you can stand behind the airborne water and look
  out
To see the clear green limestone pool and the bouldered, shaded
  canyon below.
Downstream a desert war rages, rifles fire and bombs send sand
  high in plumes.
Beside the corpses burned-out tanks and humvees litter the dry
  killing field.

Caney Creek cascades for fifty feet, white as a bridal veil, stepping
  bright
Down into clean, smooth water where mosses grow close to their
  bankside hosts.
Above, on the rim, the same outrageous war sends up toxic smoke
  and fire.
Dirty, gaunt faces of young soldiers look down on the oasis
  where we idly saunter.

"Why do the heathen rage?" they seem to ask us, knowing who
  we are.
"And why do you fail to rage when you can see us afraid, suffering
  and dying?"
We are the heathen, even as we admire these icons of Edenic
  innocence,
We are the guilty who cannot flee into wilderness deep enough
  for absolution.

Mary Carol Moran

Alabama Dog

Gemma used to be wild,
a river dog culled from a culvert under
highway 49. We sleep in a
farmhouse built on a foundation
of adzed timbers, a house of old
books. When daylight rouses me
from night sweats and I
mutter, "It can't be morning,"
when Gemma howls with a passing train
and the mail truck honks
as it backs into a cold slot—
then I remember that there are things we have forgotten,
the smell of blood,
white fragment of bone,
forest dew, the silence of the moon,
and hunger.

She only hunts in the early morning,
a black cloud drifting over grass,
her kitchen filled with gleaming knives.
She carries her kill to the dining room
where the ceiling fan whirs, my dining
room too, replete with roses and broccoli,
tomatoes and tall glasses of water,
a brocade curtain, a lithograph
by Lebadang, *epouve artist*, a room
where a vegetarian eats side by side
with a river dog, a room with heavy oak chairs
and a blood-stained carpet.

I walk through the pre-dawn
toward the bathroom, barefoot, chilled,
heavy with sleep and rebirth,
dragging a satchel of stony phrases
snagged from a dream of forgetting, forgetting
a crucial word. I see the shape first, dim
in the non-light, a branch towed inside for gnawing,
then small greasy mounds, another twig,
a slim gray toothpick. I pull the light chord
and find an ear, a meaty spine. I sniff,
wait for tears or a churned stomach. Instead
I am engulfed by a river, a river
that swallows gristle and fur,
muscle, heart, bone
and hunger.

Gemma sleeps bloated on the back porch.
I clear her remnants, scrub her woolen plate.
I crouch beside her, stroke her neck.
If we wandered the forest, it would be she
feeding me.

Jim Murphy

Almost Georgic, Alabama

A young sorrel horse runs the fenceline,
great cords of muscle gather and release

floods of energy and acid—blood's light
clarified, its soul grown huge with speed.

Earth-red, set just above the shock-green
rolling pasture, momentary Spiritus Mundi—

the close and symbiotic presence bends
my dog's small will and mine from exercise.

Destinations fused for a few tight seconds,
five thousand years' geometry draws each

figure to the others—blink, step, breath—
to own and never know—to sprint in track

shoes, pant at the end of a leash, or graze
a barrier of metal tubes—in a flash of turf

and sunlight these natures practically collide,
each sure of its exact position and capacity.

To puzzle, to hunt, to flee—shared survival
strategies, homologous as bones and teeth.

I'm advised by horse and pointer, lectured
by insects, corrected by heat waves rippling

in the road's gray grip—what I had believed
part of the earth is atmosphere, as a flock

takes its tree aloft for one long moment
after the shotgun. A technique to cultivate

the spirit—turn the earth twice over, try to
learn all lore of the domestic. Failing this,

in late husbandry of the land, use muscle
memory, and, when thinned or broken,

the tracery each beat and breath provides.

Patricia Sammon

Alabama Wetlands

"These grasses are actually quite busy," the tour guide tells us,
directing our attention to an arm-sweep of estuary shivering
       in the sunlight.
We learn that merely by idling here, in acres of slimy tangle,
several different rivers are being forgiven their heavy metals.

"And do you hear those loud clicks and pops?"
I had not,—but now they are all I can hear.
"Pistol shrimp," she tells us. "Underwater, that sound is so loud
the prey is stunned, making it easier to capture."

Next, the guide speaks of long ago, when people, driven to despair
       by malaria
discovered how to crumble the leaves of the oleander bush
and brew a deadly tea by which to escape this place.
"Here." She points out the pink blooms,—flourishing within
       arm's reach.

Next she muses upon how hard it must have been to be
       a woman here,
two hundred years ago, when this whole place was
       an indigo plantation.
Obediently we look out across the murk, and gulping, yes, we see
the throb of bent backs, the flash of iron shackles,
the viper whips, the alligator overseers.
One low groan moves across the matted expanse,
through the mud-suck of uncertain currents.

She rolls her eyes. "I mean, can you *believe* it!"
"Even in this heat, a lady couldn't go out of doors—
not without a long-sleeved, full-length dress,
       complete with petticoats
and a whale-bone corset and parasol, for goodness sakes."
Stunned, we stare at her. The marsh grasses shudder once,
letting ignorance settle into innocence.

A snowy egret angles itself through the air, by neat degrees,
the way a woman will stretch her fingers into linen gloves.
The swamp, which accommodates infinitely,
makes room for a finely-dressed woman
who has lost each of her babies to fevers, and has
in ladylike sips, swallowed the poison tea.
The bird settles in the lowest branch of a cypress,
folding itself like hands upon a lap.

We grip our handlebars and set off, single file, to the next place
    on the map.
The wetlands soak up the panting sounds of our having to catch up
and the various rusted sounds of our gears and pedals
so as to provide just enough distracting rustle
that a runaway, escaping into the canebrake,
can find the path.

Andrew Saunders

A Classic Look at Ivan, the Storm

Like Beowulf's Grendel, Ivan lurks
Reported by far off villagers and kinsman
To be fierce beyond belief
And sudden, overwhelming all defenses

Grendel's wrath is accounted beastly
Unquenchably savage, unrelenting, otherworldly
What desire, what vengeance, what deity
Shapes such horrific deeds

He tears open dens of nobles and commoners alike
Who lift their swords and shields in brave gesture
Afore he rips them limb by limb
And storms off hungrily to find more victims

He holds the world enthralled
As men think only of Grendel's threat
Numbed by fear, dispirited by void of hope
The brave are diminished, the weak paralyzed

Grendel's power grows
Without regard for plaintive supplications
Courageous acts
Or totem gods of men

Kate Seawell

Brown Pelicans

Katrina comes and goes
And these small deaths
Are not noted by NBC.

Someone, maybe it was Trey,
Said that pelicans mate for life
And along the Mobile Bayway
Brown pelicans glide
Over a highway littered with
Pelican death.
Brown pelicans glide
And in mid-flight their relation
To the dinosaur is keen.
They await the resurrection
And fly until they die
Waiting for their loved ones to rise up.

Body and body
And carcass and carcass
These small deaths
Are not reported by CNN.

First cousins to the Bergen-Belsen denizens
Of the Ninth Ward,
They, too, wait for someone to come
And get them, relieve them,
Say it's a bad dream
A mistake of true
Color blindness.

Brown pelicans
Brown bodies
Why can't we be safe
in our habitats, tonight?
Brown pelican
Rise up and fight against
The Wind and the Water.
Your passing is noted,
Your passing is mourned
By fellow brown birds
Who can't live without you
Who will circle and glide until
They, too, collapse on the Bayway
A sad heap of feathered light bones
And mourned by me,
A passenger in a green pick-up truck traveling
East towards Florida
And no more power outages.

Glenda Richmond Slater

Beach Cocoon

It has endured for
fifty years,
used seldom now
and with nostalgic care.

Upon its terry terrain
long-legged spear-throwers still run
thick elephant trunks still sway
giraffe necks endlessly intertwine.

The edges are frayed
as are my senses
but colors resonate
like the memory

Of lying on my stomach
burrowing into the softness of its African landscape
Gulf sand crunching underneath
molding

to fit my body
feeling moisture and grit
smelling salty spray.
Lulled by liquid sound rolling in, rolling out.
Giving up my self to Alabama heat

In my beach cocoon.

R.T. Smith

Jubilee

Some nights in the summer months
sea creatures crawl up on the beach.
Old folks claim they can predict
Science can't tell us a thing.
On the east shore of Mobile Bay
I have seen perch, snapper, and flounder
flip like jewels on the sand,
shrimp and manta ray dance
like celebrating natives,
a crab gone mad with something
in his blood he could not name
try to climb a tree,
as if evolution were trying to prove
itself in one crazed migration.
We all ran down to the tide's leavings,
boots on and the blue gigs flashing
barbed tines as if to keep the ocean
from changing its mind about the gift.
We collected the insane bounty
and marveled at the sharpened moon
as cook fires lit up the beach.
So we feasted upon the manna cast
on sand, sang the season,
danced the steps of our ancestors
and slept the sleep of men
who have touched the source of dreams. [7]

Betty Spence

Blackberry Picking 101

On the campus of South Alabama
a sudden start of summer rain
pushes me past a hillside in berry.
As if turning from green to red,
red to purple-black just like that . . .
and that just for me, blackberries
holler out: "Wade in and start picking."

Berrying is a matter of touch and take,
you know. At the slightest fingering
black satin berries sweetly let go.
With all the feelings of the body spreading
like wild fire to finger's tipmost ends,
without being taught, fingers know
when fruits of the earth are ripe.

Like Stafford wincing his way wildly
from impulse to impulse, passing himself
back and forth through the bramble-cure,
I follow the trailings-up; the climbings-down
of the Rubus, the Trivialis,
and find momentary stays purpling
on the ground beneath my feet.

Catherine A. Swender

Spanish Moss

Spanish Moss hanging on ancient oaks
Tells me of my future.

My body, used to cold,
Withers in a heat that is not mine,
A Midwesterner living in Mobile.

There is something older, wilder
In this place
Where morning comes fiercely
Wakes me from dreams of autumn,
And the promise of apples in cool September.

Here, the air is so rich
You don't need roots to thrive.

Still, there is something ghostly
About these tendrils of Spanish Moss
Dangling from branches of old oak trees
Swaying in the breeze off Mobile Bay
Needing no land to be home.

Seth Tanner

Painted Turtle

I launch my kayak
into Choccolocco Creek
with only inches to
spare, paddle serving
as pole much of the
time. Every Easter
water fills the lowlands
changing creeks, bogs
and marshes into
backwater fisheries.
The gar are spawning.
They walk on invisible legs,
splashing and thrashing
about in Bacchanalian
delight.   Adrift in
this primeval orgy, I
back-paddle to avoid
a rock. The vessel veers,
flowing just to its left.
Looking down at my
obstruction, I see a
distinct yellow stripe.
Bubbles emerge from the
murk—carapace covered
in lake-bottom mud,
not one scute distinguishable
from the other. Still floating,
I look over my shoulder.
You have risen to the surface—
your first breath of
spring. The kayak stalls. I
wonder if the gar woke you,
or if the water, a slow suction,
forced you from your muddy slumber.

Peggy Teel

Pink Pelican

Pink Pelican at the Pointe
serves up sunsets with seafood and sandwiches on sourdough;
pelicans perch atop pilings, staring into the water,
waiting for fish that evaded the chef's pot;
margarita glasses sweat in sunshine's heat,
wondering where Buffet went and if he'll return
to watch the sun sink into the Bay;
girls in shorts and tee shirts
deliver shrimp platters and beer to locals
while vacationers lick salt from glasses
like the one Jimmy left behind.

Margaret J. Vann

Little River Lily

I.

(A group of four
looking for the wildflower)

The trip to DeSoto was uneventful;
we hiked the Cascade Trail
found the pink lady's slipper,
fringed phacelia, Iris verna
(a most successful walk).

I had promised a special view
and Widow's cross. We drove to
Little River Canyon
for the view and the flowers.

At the limestone shelf,
I was on my knees
examining some small thing
(I've forgotten what).

I heard a sharp hiss and looked up
over there—there from the woods
emerged a bearded man.

He wore hat and boots.
We stared mouths agape
as he strode toward us.
(It is funny the details one remembers.)

He wore hat and boots unlaced.
Frozen we mumbled among us
as we watched him move
in our direction.

He wore a beard and hat and boots unlaced.
I knelt there behind the unleaved blueberry bush
my friends touching my shoulder.
(Why can't I remember the flower?)

He passed us by
dressed in beard, rawhide hat, unlaced boots, and a tan.
(I *had* promised a special view.)

II.

(Years later with other friends
for other reasons)

The lecturer spoke of the
Trail of Tears and his journey to
adopt the heritage of his ancestors.

He spent his time in the beloved woods of
those Cherokee
who had escaped the soldiers and the walk.

I see his bearded face and rawhide hat
on a book jacket.
(He is a regional author.)

He looks familiar.

Later
I remember unlaced boots
and the tan.

VII.

History Remembers

Helen Blackshear

Muskogee Legacy

Indian names fall softly on the tongue—
Eufaula, Chattahoochee, Tuscaloosa,
Tuskegee, Talledega, Tallapoosa.
Like chuckling creeks that ran among
the hills and valleys when the state was young
they echo in our ear; Abbacoochee,
Hatchechubee, Cherokee, and Uchee
sigh through the trees where once their songs were sung.

We banished them, save for one struggling band,
into the west along the Trail of Tears,
their fate almost forgotten through the years,
sad victims of the settlers' greed for land.

Though shameful sorrows haunt their history,
those lovely names they left as legacy.

Diann Blakely

Little Boy Blue

Faint echoes rise from graves. Full moon, midnight.
Your teacher, Ike, last played in Alabama.
Little Boy Blue, please come blow your horn:

You listen, turn the new song *round and round.*
O turn it round then finger those harsh dates
Carved into rock. Into wood crosses, slanted

On this flood plain down by the western tracks
The boxcars gulp, rattling through kudzu
Like a giant snake. *Please come blow your horn,*

Ike sings, but history shakes with louder sounds
As midnight turns back into blood-moist drama
And you can almost hear the river, torn

By mortar fire. Does Ike hear it too?
You've both jumped trains to Vicksburg, its bluffs high
And ruined with the shelled townhomes of planters,

The broken columns veiled in river-mist
Like this, mist white as a hoop-skirt, or shroud.
O dig your fingers deep, o turn them round

Till you see gunboats, see besieged families crawl
From caves carved into mud, swapping mad fists
Over hardtack and rat meat. O see men fall

And see them march, most uniformed in blue—
Come blow your horn—till you echo God's hiss
And dead slaves' laughter, shaking dirt-chained bones. [1]

Robert Collins

The Antichrist in Alabama

You have to begin somewhere,
the Antichrist explains,
and what better place to start from
than the rough and tumble state
of mind called Alabama,
where politics is never really local.

Disguised as any ordinary Bubba,
good ole boy armed with the good
book and sporting a bad comb-over
to cover up the number of the beast,
he's far less likely to be recognized
for who and what he really is.

Because it takes all Ten Commandments
to get his name on ballots and elected,
his overconfident opponents
don't respect him, but he aims to see
the ancient prophecies fulfilled
and all his dreams come true.

Before the general public knows it,
just as his political career seems to lie
in ruins, with one eye on the White House,
he occupies the mansion in Montgomery,
consolidates his power, redecorates,
pushes the Pledge of Allegiance

and prayer in school, keeps taxes
low and games of chance illegal.
When the upstate intellectuals attack,
he seizes free time on APT and makes
fun of evolution, so Christians
everywhere will love him.

Until it's too late to recover,
his liberal enemies don't realize
who they're actually dealing with—
what tough sob, his quarter hour
come round at last, slouches toward
Birmingham, claiming he's reborn.

Michael S. Harper

American History

for John Callahan

Those four black girls blown up
in that Alabama church
remind me of five hundred
middle passage blacks,
in a net, under water
in Charleston harbor
so *redcoats* wouldn't find them.
Can't find what you can't see
can you? [2]

Dorothy Diemer Hendry

Mama's New Gown

Alabama is like a beautiful woman with nothing to wear but
a bulky gown constituted of patches and tatters.
When she tries to move forward, the patches
weigh her down and the tatters tangle her feet.
Her sister states laugh whenever she stumbles.
"Poor thing! Why does she wear that raggedy old dress?
She's her own worst enemy."

Fortunately Alabama has many children who love her.
Some of them say, "We like Mama in her old dress.
Some of the patches are sacred."

Other children say, "Mama deserves something better.
Let's go to Montgomery and design it."

The end of the story could be that beautiful Alabama
would step forth in a svelte new gown.
Undoubtedly the gown would have spiritual motifs
woven into its durable fabric, but it would also have
ergonomic lines, enabling Alabama to move freely
and to work harmoniously with any or all of her children.
Alabama's sister states would exclaim, "Look at Alabama
in her bright new gown! Whoever thought
she could be so stunning?"

All of us who are Alabama's children would smile
and declare proudly, "That's our mama! We're
moving with her to the front of the line!"

Jennifer Horne

WPA

Hey Walker, hey Jim, you did good,
you did what you could in the time
you had to say what had to be said.
Tell me, was that God walking barefoot down the road?
We went by so fast I hardly saw him.

Some of us here
don't know whether
to save it
or let it go.
We want
a history
and it's the only one
we've got.

Why look back? It's over.

Where do we go from here?

Sometimes I think I'll have to leave.

Old Joe Clark he had a house,
forty stories high,
and every story in that house
was filled with chicken pie.
Fare thee well, Old Joe Clark,
Fare thee well, I say.
Fare thee well, Old Joe Clark,
Better be on my way.

Oh, it's not just
the white neoclassical columns,
the black jockey hitching post in the front yard,
not the Confederate battle flag bumper sticker,

or boys in the bar singing "Sweet Home Alabama,"
or even the way the "did-you-hear-about-the-gentleman-
    of-the-colored-persuasion-who"
jokes get brought out as soon as it's just us white folks.
    "Oh shit, I just forgot she was in the room."
    "I forgot she was black."
    "Do you think she— ?"
    "No, I don't think so."
It's not the apart it's the together,
not the separate it's the connect.
It was working side by side in the field,
it's playing softball on a hot July day,
and if all our sweat isn't the same,
salt and water, just like our tears,
well I'll be a monkey's uncle.

Meat & three,
meat & three,
meat & three
at the City Cafe.

In the evenin' by the moonlight,
you could hear the darkies singin'.
In the evenin' by the moonlight,
you could hear their banjoes ringin'.
How the old folks would enjoy it,
they would sit all night and listen,
as they sang in the evenin' by the moonlight.
Ladidoodah, ladidoodah,
ladidoodee, ladidoodee, ladidoodah.

This is clear:
pure hate is easy,
pure heat, pure hate is clarifying,
even dressed up in a David Duke suit
like a hot knife through butter
wouldn't melt in his mouth.

As if poison ivy, chiggers, ticks,
water moccasins, fire ants,
rattlesnakes and a hundred degrees

at 6 a.m. in the shade weren't enough.

I love the South.
I love the South not.
And so on until the ground is littered with petals.

A dogtrot is both the cabin
and the passage down its center,
a breezeway to past and future,
the one hard, the other uncertain.
Some evenings it's a cool haven,
the loud hum of cicadas,
one lone frog piping hopefully into the night
fit accompaniment for a quiet mind.

June slid by like a dream
       of dripping trees,
         something that slips your mind
         upon waking,
         though its mood remains,
         sleep-suffused, shaded,
         a bit warm for comfort.

This piney woods clearing,
this green heaven
where we lay down together,
sun filtering through the leaves—
we could have been the only two people on earth,
Adam and Eve all over,
but without the sinning.
If that *was* sin,
let's do it again.

Down in the valley,
valley so low,
hang your head over,
hear the wind blow.
Hear the wind blow, dear,
hear the wind blow.
Hang your head over,
hear the wind blow.

Jim wrote:
"Pinned all along the edge of this mantel, a broad fringe of white tissue paper which Mrs. Gudger folded many times on itself and scissored into pierced geometrics of lace, and of which she speaks as her last effort to make this house pretty."

A dead pine with hollow gourds hanging
against a clouded sky
is what? A warning,
a metaphor, a minor collage,
a habit? Or what it is:
a home for martins,
an invitation to nest
from people who know something about migration.

Sometimes on Sundays at my grandmother's house
after church, still wearing our starched dresses,
our patent leather shoes,
we'd beg to drive past the crazyman's house
on the outskirts of town,
his yard and home a kaleidoscope
of hubcaps and blue bottles,
old tires painted white,
crazy-quilt paths lined with rocks.
Each time, seeing him sitting on his porch
as we drove slowly past,
I'd feel a sudden flush of shame,
his creation on display for gaping children.

On the way home:
Well, it rained all night the day I left,
the weather it was dry,
the sun so hot I froze to death,
Susannah, don't you cry.

In 1936, Bill's father
worked for the Sunshine Bakery
and had to borrow money
to pay for his son's birth.
I'd say he was worth it,
wouldn't you, Mr. Christenberry?

Nowhere have I seen them.
Like Citizens Councils and swastikas,
they are stories in a book,
pictures caught by flashbulbs,
an old bad smell, an obscene wink.
I sense them as echoes, smoke from a doused fire:
here on Highway 11 is where the sign was,
this was the restaurant they met in,
this the courthouse where Christenberry
saw the masked face.
And here in Mobile is where the young man was lynched,
and here is the judge who made them bankrupt.
Would you want to see a cross burning
in someone's front yard, if you could?
I wonder, from my peaceful room,
if I would have been brave in those wars.

Harper's: "By 1859 northern manufacture provided an annual return of $1.9 billion, while southern agriculture yielded only $204 million; all that remained to be discussed was whether the political revolution evident in the arithmetic would find expression as a treaty of peace or an act of war."

Well, I fight
against being polemical.
Still, where else
did all that wealth
come from
but free labor?

You can drive down roads
for miles on end, interrupted only
by a deer leaping ahead of the car,
legs outstretched
as in a woodland frieze.
Here, in summer,
are seasonal cathedrals
green transepts,
tumbling buttresses
contrived of heart-shaped leaves
that die to rise again

and hide, deep-shadowed,
a secret clustered purple flower.
On a lucky day you see
a kingfisher dive into still water,
dead pines poking up like fingers,
hear the low repeated cry of a bittern.
The trees have seen it all,
have even been implicated in death,
but sunlight slants equally through their branches
on evil or beauty,
and this is some kind of consolation.

I confess I'm uneasy
in these mansion-museums,
monuments to gracious living,
the style of which—
someone is saying
this is her "idea of Heaven"
and it's true the view
over these sloping fields is *magnificent*
until the docent tells us
how it helped the master
keep an eye on his slaves.
Ah, the uses of beauty.
Here is the very telescope with which—

From the raised and crumbling porch
of Saunders Hall, its cotton fields
stretching flat as a coverlet
and descendants of sharecroppers
in the decaying big house
who overlook them.
"I grew up in this house,"
he says. "And one day some men
from the Saunders family came
and took the headstones
out of the family graveyard.
One of 'em left his glasses
lyin' on the ground,
and me and daddy jumped in the truck
and caught up with 'em.

I remember that."
Let's have another Bloody Mary
from the cocktail tables set up in the yard
and try to ignore the woman
with her head wrapped in a bandage
as though just returned from battle.
It was she who planted the flowers by the steps.
See, the dirt's still freshly turned.

No matter how long I live here
I don't think I'll understand it all
so why keep banging my head against it?
Go to Wal-Mart
and see, there, how a bargain
breaks down barriers to integration.
E pluribus unum, y'all.

Mr. Frog went a'courtin', he did ride, umhmmm, umhmm.
Mr. Frog went a'courtin', he did ride, umhmmm, umhmm.
Mr. Frog went a'courtin', he did ride, sword and a pistol
    by his side,
Mr. Frog went a'courtin', he did ride, umhmmm.

Sometimes on the porch late at night,
everybody tired from the day's work,
talking about how it might be a good year, this time,
this time we might get ahead, for once,
she'd sit in her momma's lap,
too big for it now but allowed,
on a night like this,
and dream her way into a future
where she'd be a nurse, or maybe a teacher,
and live in a nice house with curtains,
and maybe a good stove,
and there would be a man
much like her daddy but dressed in a suit,
and he would love her.

I see the moon and the moon sees me,
the moon sees somebody I'd like to see.
God bless the moon and God bless me,
God bless somebody I'd like to see.

If everyone falls silent
at twenty minutes before or after the hour,
an angel is passing over the house.

Itchy nose: company coming.
Dropped spoon: the same.
Set an extra place.

Shiver down your spine:
Rabbit ran over your grave.
Rabbit ran over your grave.

The black man on the riverwalk
asks for spare change.
People are afraid.
They have their wallets to protect,
their sense of safety.
"Spare change? For a cup of coffee?
Hey. Hey! This ain't the wind talkin'."

So often we misunderstand:
Anne Sexton wrote she was "on tender hooks."
The woman with the magic magnets in her shoes
says, "These are in the form of insults,
but they come in all kinds."
And those three families
Jim and Walker befriended
believed their lives would be changed
because, because how could they not?
This was momentous
for someone to pay them this kind of attention.
For the better?

*She'll be comin' round the mountain
when she comes.
She'll be comin' round the mountain
when she comes.
She'll be comin' round the mountain,
she'll be comin' round the mountain,
she'll be comin' round the mountain,
when she comes.*

At the roadside stand:
"Hot Jumbo Boiled Peanuts—
Regular or Cajun."

And I remember
stopping beside the highway
to pick a boll of cotton
and how far we'd come
from my father's boyhood,
his skin itchy from picking peaches all day,
his overalls—the symbol of their poverty—
heavy with sweat.
What a curiosity to us:
cotton in its raw form,
ragged white puff on a brown stem,
long before it became
the Buster Brown t-shirts and shorts and socks
we picked out at the Heights Variety dime store.

A partial reading list:

*All God's Dangers
Let Us Now Praise Famous Men
Absalom, Absalom!
Gone With the Wind
Jubilee
A Childhood
To Kill a Mockingbird*

And if I read all the books,
then will it all make sense?

Come with me.
We'll start in the chalky loam
of the Black Belt
and follow the ocean's path
down to the Gulf.
You bring the beer,
I'll bring the salt-and-vinegar chips
and we'll play hookey together
on the first day of spring.
I can feel the sand now,
gritty and cool
on the soles of my feet,
and if the water's too chilly
to immerse ourselves just yet,
we'll walk awhile,
maybe as far as Perdido Pass.

Here, in this open book of sea and sand,
I can imagine a change of heart—
in the old tradition, sudden and lasting.
This is what I, who don't pray, pray for:
something new, out of the clear blue sky.

Ruth Gunter Mitchell

The Powers That Tried

They issued masks, duct tape, and maps for escape.
They reminded us the winds could blow Sarin to our zone.
They declared PCBs pollute our water and soil.
They warned airborne shrills of sirens save lives.

They forgot we were neighbors before we were victims.
Our infected sore is home where we live and work.
We grow our blueberries and tomatoes in this dirty dirt.
We rear our children and educate, not contaminate, them.

We covet a future without masks, duct tape, and maps,
A future without poisonous gases and fumes,
A future without fatal creeks, gray air and dead fish,
A future, most of all, without the stench of them.

We reclaim our backyard barbeques and hikes through the
    woods,
Our gardens and churches and children on playgrounds,
Our proud parades and pageantry and festivals with hope,
Our paychecks from our jobs, not from lawsuits.

Maybe we suffered from cancer of skin, organs and tissue,
Yet, no malignancy assaulted nor nibbled at our spirits.
We survived, we sanitized, and we remained proud.
We are Anniston, and on sacred soil we withstand!

Minnie Bruce Pratt

On the Road to Selma

"[In 1955, during the Montgomery bus boycott mass arrests], Blacks had come from every section of town. Black women with bandannas on, wearing men's hats with their dresses rolled up. From the alleys they came, that is what frightened white people. Not the collar and tie group. I walked in there and the cops were trembling. . . . One of the police hollered, 'All right, you women get back' These *great big old women* told him, and I never will forget their language, 'Us ain't going nowhere. You done arrested us preachers and we ain't moving. He put his hands on his gun and his club. They said, 'We don't care what you got. If you hit one of us, you'll not leave here alive.'" — B. J. Simms

In her birthplace, she's a tourist in the shrine to martyrs
for freedom, votive lights set before photographs,
newspaper names: Reeb, Liuzzo, Jimmie Lee Jackson.
Under the flicker of their stubborn eyes, she fingers
bare footprints, plaster casts on a museum table,
steps of unknown travelers set down by the riverside.
Those who climbed and crossed the bridge: maidservant,
carpenter, teacher, fieldhand, and no way to tell
who was who, no match between work and foot. Naked,
ready for cool water in a tin basin, someone to wash
off the dust. How beautiful upon the mountain the feet
of them that bring good. Arc of flesh heavy in her hand.

    She has a dream sometimes she is walking the road
    out of town, past the depot and the gin, on the road
    to Selma, past burnt-up fields. The jaybird declares
    to the crow. *Rain no more*, and the dry creek crawls.
    Catfish gasp for breath, but the crawfish steadily
    dredge the world up, scratching clay from underneath.

Going downhill she pours shade like water on her head,
slides her bare arm past briar jaws to pick dewberries.
Knife vines slit her skin, but each berry's a rough nipple
in her mouth, lost bliss. Kiss of memory sunk in her flesh,
imprint, sure as clay holds each foot ever on it, toes splayed
or heel of boot.

                She tastes the music a long ways off
as doors open, voices come down the road. She can almost
grasp the meaning, echo of people bound for the meeting.

      We jumped rope with bramble briars, we'd peel
the thorns right off.
                  In a little while gonna
turn back to dirt, don't matter how rich, we be
nothin but dirt.

                Worked for a lady once, she
was sweet, she was mud rich, so when everyone be
                gone,
and everything, she lost her mind over that land.
She said, We couldn't keep our place, our place.

      Worked for a lady once, she played bridge, she sat
on her sofa to read poetry, didn't know we had
the same thing under our skirts.

                In our house, the hens
pecked through the floor cracks. I kept baby in a pasteboard
box under the gumtree. Water at noon.
Thank mercy, couldn't ever dip that spring dry.

I've tried to live a life I'm not ashamed of. A lie is
a lie, don't matter how you dress it up. I'm not
ashamed for my life to be on the air. Can you say that?

Beatrice follows behind, comes on three buzzards sitting
in the road. They grunt and hiss and flap. They rip some life
from a small dead animal, stinking, past.
                                                The field's
bone-dry, not enough water at the river to swim a dog.
Tracks at the water's edge, confusion, the mud-split hooves
of cows, come to drink and trample marks where people waded
out, no sure place where she can set her feet.

    A voice calls back her way, *Soon we all gonna be
dirt, nothin but dirt, might as well join us.*

    They say, *Are you ready to sleep in a cardboard box
on the cold clay ground, are you ready to stand ready
while we speak from a platform of coffins? Are you ready
to walk?*

               The road turns. She turns aside, down a worn path
under barbwire. A Black man leaves as she sneaks through,
says, *No matter what, they'll say I raped you.* His foot and hand
stretch the fence jaws for her passage. *They'll tell you how often.
Forty-seven times. Remember I told you.*

                            Property line.
While stile steps at another fence. Dirt road by the quarters,
paved road by the courthouse. In front the white men laugh,
No way out, you slut. Hands on their crotches, forking roads.

    The road to Snow Hill where William Edwards walks to
        school
with bare bleeding feet, praying, *Summer, please come, wild
    plums.*

    The road to Camp Hill where Ralph Gray stands with his
        shotgun
to guard the meeting place, vacant house in a cotton field.
Only the bloom of yellow eyes watch when the sheriff
    comes.

       The road through Lowndes County, coming up on a car
           slewed
across. Through the mesh of broken glass the white
           woman's
blasted eyes search blindly for the dark riders she ferried,
can they reach safety?

             Beatrice wants to be, wants to be, wants to be
ready. The road through the courthouse, the room where her father
stands over her as she marks her ballot. White rooster. Black
panther. Somewhere in this long hall a hidden door.
A woman hauling a tin pail of water points, *Yes.*

         Past her, the museum of shadows.
Light opens. A woman leaves, says, *I lived this, I can't watch it.*
The video whirs, pours out black-and-white people stumbling.

Through the window she sees rain come up a river that splits
and shakes like a leaf as the gulf wind hits it.

               She sees children
beaten by fists of water. She sees people climb a mountain bridge
to stand in mist, tear gas, men on horseback with cattle prods.
The woman in the hallway whispers, *One way in, and one way out.*

Past the blank screen, she sees the other side of the water,
the riverbank and people gathered. Are they her people? Can't
see their faces. Once she ran here falling on soft grass, darkness.
The only light, fireflies and fire under iron cook kettles. Hot grease
smell, the promise of food for all, crisp fish. Glimmer of faces bent
over flame, marking her in place. Once. Once in the morning
      sunflash
she ran down to swim, and strangers stood knee-deep singing,
      Come,
in the muddy water, a song she knew, from unknown mouths. Now

this silent room. Lightning flickers in the storm's stern grasp. Gutteral thunder in the river's throat, echo of an old song. Woman, men, children march under torchlight, hoes and shovels for weapons, the rusty blades, and bare feet dusty from the field. They cross the river and sing, *Arise, ye slaves no more in thrall. Prisoners of starvation*, their hungry mouths chew the bloody word, *Arise.* [3]

James Miller Robinson

At Big Spring Park

An empty picnic table sits beside the clear
slow-moving current of Indian Creek cotton canal
with its stone walls shaped and placed by slaves
a hundred and eighty years ago
when a handful of planters, brokers, and bankers
saw the need to expedite the loading of their bales
onto steamboats at the Tennessee River ten miles away.
It took hundreds of them
with shovels and picks keeping time
with mournful songs and buckets full of dirt and sweat
eleven years to complete the project
with dozens of long-eared mules hitched to wagons
half-asleep and staring down between their blinders
at the chip and crack of iron and rock.
It took half a century more to erect the blocks
of mansions that sprouted along the cobblestone streets
behind white columns, closed windows and thick doors.
A hundred years later they landscaped a park
around the squirting spring and along the banks
of the canal all the way to the rounded ponds it feeds.
They brought white geese, ducks and swans to glide
like angels across the crystal surface of the dark water.
The giant carp they stocked grew
and multiplied amid the bundling water weed.
Unforgetting willow trees sprouted up
to weep and sway at the edges of the ponds.
If you listen hard when the traffic subsides
and the chirping birds roost
in the upper branches of the trees,
you can still hear the mournful sound
of slaves shifting shovels back and forth,
lifting iron picks and slamming them down.

Christopher Singleton

The Typewriter
once Hitler's, now in the Hall of History, Bessemer, Alabama

We are the guardians
   of antique iniquity,
      the cancer of mortals,
         the inherent perils of humanity.
The sodden, rusted
   once bold, swift vehicle
      of the surest threat
         mankind ever knew of itself.
            Words of greed.
            Sermons of hate.
            Pledges of death.
         Lamentations from the cold, hard heart
      of a great evil once loosed upon the earth.
Seal it away!
   And here it stays, buried
        in the heart of a fertile fortress—
   a city in the north
      forged in cold, hard steel—
   where few are wise
      to its existence still.
Look, but don't touch!
   Save your fingers from that polished poison
      where his lay down and rapped out
    his genocidal abominations, founded in masses
    his man-made plague.
Yes, for all our sakes, do look!
   Hear its wounded weeping.
     Feel of its pain.
      Learn from its strife.
   But fear it not,
      for we are the guardians.

Notes and Acknowledgments

I. Places Remember

(1) **Ray Bradbury**: Written sometime before 1978, when the author was travelling from Los Angeles to Atlanta by train, for a Science Fiction convention. Passing through Tuscaloosa, he saw the old slogan, "The Druid City." It was a puzzlement to him, since the Druids are the stuff of mythology and fantasy. It made him wonder about what lay beneath the underbelly of Tuscaloosa." — From *The Haunted Computer And The Android Pope*, Knopf, 1981

(2) **Tom Drinkard**: from *Finding the Way Home.*

(3) **John Finlay**: from *Mind and Blood*, John Daniel & Company, 1992; permission to reprint granted by Jean Finlay.

(4) **Andrew Hudgins**: from *Babylon In A Jar.*

(5) **Susan Luther**: first published in *Poem*; repeated in *Alabama Poets* and *Breathing in the Dark.*

(6) **James Mersmann**: from *Straying Toward Home*, Court Street Press.

(7) **Mary Murphy**: from *Literary Mobile*, Negative Capability Press.

(8) **Thomas Rabbitt**: from *Prepositional Heaven*, River City Publishing.

(9) **Donna Jean Tennis**: from *Love on Wry*, Professional Touch.

(10) **Jeanie Thompson**: This poem was previously published in the online journal *Thicket* (www.athicket.com) in a slightly different form. It is included in a manuscript called *Cinemagraphique* which is currently under consideration.

(11) **Miller Williams**: from *Some Jazz a While: Collected Poems.* Copyright 1999 by Miller Williams. Used with permission of the poet and the University of Illinois Press.

II. People Remember

(1) **Richard G. Beyer**: from *The Panhandler*, #25, Spring 1992.

(2) **Rita Dove**: From *On The Bus With Rosa Parks*, Copyright © 1999 by Rita Dove. Used by permission of W.W. Norton & Company, Inc.

(3) **Anne George**: From *Some of it is True*, Curbow Publications.

(4) **Peter Huggins**: from *Hard Facts*, Livingston Press.

(5) **Rodney Jones**: published in *The Unborn*, Atlantic Monthly Press, and *Salvation Blues: 100 Poems*, Houghton Mifflin.

(6) **Jim Simmerman**: from *Once Out of Nature*.

(7) **Julie Suk:** from *The Medicine Woman*, St. Andrews Press; "Floating Island" was a Mobile, Alabama, woman wandering to find her lost lover.

(8) **Sue Brannan Walker**: Italicized passage is from E. O. Wilson's *Naturalist*. This poem was previously published in *ISLE:* Vol. 13.2 (Summer 2006).

III. Music Remembers

(1) **John T. Morris**: from *Burning Time*.

IV. Seasons Remember

(1) **J. William Chambers**: from *Collage: A Tribute to Steven Owen Bailey*, Negative Capability Press, 2006.

(2) **Abram Ryan**: from the poem "Last of May" in *Poems: Patrotic, Religious, Miscellaneous.*, New York: P.J. Kenedy And Sons, 1880.

V. Yesterday Remembers

(1) **Margaret Cutchins**: from *Ladders We Climb to Who We Are*, Holly Creek Press.

(2) **James Dickey**: Copyright © 1965 by James Dickey, First printed in *The New Yorker.* Reprinted with permission of McIntosh & Otis, Inc.

(3) **John Hafner**: Korbett's Bar was in Mobile, Alabama.

(4) **Marjorie Lees Linn**: from *Threads from Silence*, Providence Press.

(5) **Joseph Sackett**: from *All the World's a Stage.*

VI. Nature Remembers

(1) **Bettye Kramer Cannizzo**: The yellowhammer or yellow-shafted flicker is the state bird of Alabama.

(2) **Mary Brobston Cleverdon**: "The cattle egret builds a small twig nest similar to that of other herons. In Alabama it most often nests in colonies of the Little Blue Heron and White Ibis, other herons and ibis, and seldom, if ever, in pure colonies. Apparently colonial birds, those which nest in large groups in close association, need the stimulus of witnessing others carrying out the various phases of the reproductive cycle."
—Thomas Imhof, *Alabama Birds*, University of Alabama Press, 1976

(3) **Dwight Eddins**:

    Naheola: Community with discontinued P.O. . . . in Choctaw County. Named for the bluff on the west bank of the Tombigbee River called *Naheola* by the Indians. . . . Choctaw *nahollo*, the source of this name, means not only 'white man' . . . but also 'something supernatural or remarkable' and was also applied to mythic beings before it was applied to white men.

    Tombigbee River: The name, derived from Choctaw *itombi* 'box, coffin' and ikbi 'makers,' refers to old men who cleaned the bones of the dead before placing these in boxes for burial. — Virginia Foscue, *Place Names in Alabama*

(4) **Charles Ghigna**: from *Speaking in Tongues: New and Selected Poems (1974-1994)*, Livingston University Press.

(5) **Dennis Hale**: The Pea River flooded Elba (usually in March) in 1865, 1888, 1929, 1938, 1959, 1975, 1990, 1994, and 1998 — Source: Wikipedia.

(6) **Tom McDougle**: from *The Eclectic Literary Forum.*

(7) **R. T. Smith**: "A jubilee is a natural phenomenon on Mobile Bay — And other places around the world — in which vast numbers of fish seem compelled by instinct or some other force to leave the water and leap onto the beaches." — From *In Our Own Words: Alabamians Read Alabama*, The Auburn University Center for the Arts & Humanities and the Alabama Cooperative Extension Service, Auburn University, 1991.

VII. *History Remembers*

(1) **Diann Blakely**: from *Rain at our Door: Duets with Robert Johnson.*

(2) **Michael S. Harper**: "American History" is a reiteration of the Oresteia in the reference to "net"; that is, the cyclic unknown history of a new nation repeating the breaking of ancient codes of incest and miscegenation; the concept is indebted to Ralph Ellison's *Invisible Man*, the novel. From *Images of Kin* by Michael S. Harper, published by University of Illinois Press. By permission of Michael S. Harper.

(3) **Minnie Bruce Pratt**: from *Walking Back Up Depot Street*, 1999, University of Pittsburgh Press. By permission of Minnie Bruce Pratt and the University of Pittsburgh Press.

Contributors

Leonard Aldes (Mobile, AL), a medical school professor, neuroscientist, & musician for over 35 years, has written poetry, lyrics & composed music for almost that long. His more recent undertaking, & by the far the most challenging, has been as a cancer survivor.

Bruce Alford (Mobile, AL) is an Assistant Professor of Creative Writing at the University of South Alabama in Mobile. He received his MFA from the University of Alabama at Tuscaloosa. His poetry, informed by a Southern Missionary Baptist tradition, often explores the tension between place & history. His book *Terminal Switching* was published in spring 2007 by Elk River Review Press.

Jane Allen (Wetumpka, AL), a retired civil service employee, writes fiction, nonfiction, & poetry & has won numerous awards. Her works have been included in state & national publications. She is a member of the Huntsville (AL) Branch, National League of American Pen Women; Alabama Writers' Conclave; & Women In The Arts (WITA, Decatur, IL).

Steve Bailey (1959-2004), artist, designer, a native of Columbia, TN, helped plan, incorporate, & start *Elk River Review* in 1990. He served as its designer, staff artist, & one of its editors. He designed covers for J. William Chambers' *A Taste of Wine and Gentian* (Negative Capability Press, 2000) & Sue Scalf's *What the Moon Knows* (Elk River Review Press, 2003).

Gerald Barrax (Raleigh, NC) is a professor of English at North Carolina State University. His books of poetry include *From a Person Sitting in Darkness: New and Selected Poems*, the Pulitzer Prize nominated *Leaning Against the Sun* & *The Deaths of Animals and Lesser Gods*. He has been a poetry editor for the journals *Obsidian* & *Callaloo*.

Frederick W. Bassett (Hilton Head, SC), a native of Roanoke, AL. His publications include: *Apostrophe, Cairn, Negative Capability, Passager, Pembroke Magazine, Plainsongs, Potato Eyes, Pudding Magazine, Savannah Literary Journal, The Cape Rock,* & *Zone 3*. He has two books of "found" poetry published by Paraclete Press: *Love: The Song of Songs* & *Awake My Heart*.

Jerri Beck (Birmingham, AL) works at a Birmingham bookstore & volunteers as a docent at the Birmingham Zoo. Her poems also draw on the lessons of words, actions, & good intentions learned growing up on a Cherokee reservation. Her unique experience & bipolar disorder lead her to ask questions, some of which lead to poems rather than answers.

Robin Behn (Tuscaloosa, AL) has received fellowships from the Guggenheim Foundation & the National Endowment for the Arts. Her collections of poetry include *Paper Bird, The Red Hour,* & *Horizon Note,* which won the 2001 Brittingham Prize in Poetry. She co-edited *The Practice of Poetry: Writing Exercises from Poets Who Teach.*

Alexis Beard (Mobile, AL) is an English major concentrating in Creative Writing at the University of South Alabama. She was born and raised in the Midwest, but came to the South to go to college in Mobile, where she currently lives & plays for the University of South Alabama Women's Golf team.

Jack B. Bedell (Hammond, LA) is a professor of English & Director of Creative Writing at Southeastern Louisiana University, where he edits Louisiana Literature & directs the Louisiana Literature Press. His most recent collection, *Come Rain, Come Shine,* was published by Texas Review Press. His poems appear regularly in *Southern Review, Hudson Review, Connecticut Review,* & other journals.

T.J. Beitelman (Birmingham, AL) has published in such journals as *Colorado Review, Quarterly West, Indiana Review,* & *New Orleans Review.* In 2002, he was awarded a fellowship in literature from the Alabama State Council on the Arts. He holds an MFA from the University of Alabama where he edited *Black Warrior Review.*

Allen Berry (Huntsville, AL) is the founder & president of the Limestone Dust Poetry Festival. He began writing at age 14 & wrote the first thing that he would share with anyone at age 23. He has lived most of his life in the state of Alabama where he spent his summers dividing his time between his father's store & his grandfather's farm.

Jake Berry (Florence, AL) is a poet, songwriter, & visual artist. His books include *Species of Abandoned Light* (Pantograph Press), *Blood Paradoxes/War Poems* (XPressEd) & *Brambu Drezi* (Barrytown/Station Hill Press). His work appears regularly in journals, magazines, & online publications. Selections of his songs are available online at music.download.com under his own name as well as under Bare Knuckles, Ascension Brothers, & Catachthonia.

Joe M. Berry (Huntsville, AL), a product of Alabama's Great Depression Years, & once a trial lawyer, is now a storyteller, volunteer teacher, & full-time iconoclast. He hopes that God will spare him the long prayers of too many preachers & the shallow talk of too many politicians, & grant him the confidence of simple people, the love of little children, & the ability to express himself in a few words.

Richard G. Beyer (Tuscumbia, AL), is the author of *The Homely Muse*, *Scrod I* (with friends), and *Profit And Loss*. His poems have appeared in over 100 poetry journals & literary magazines. He spoke often to college classes & writers' groups & gave readings of his own work & that of other Alabama poets. Founding president of the Alabama State Poetry Society from 1968 to 1970, he served on the editorial staffs of several Deep South literary publications.

Margaret Key Biggs (Heflin, AL) is a former teacher. She is a fiction writer as well as a poet & has published five books of poetry.

Helen Blackshear (1911– 2003) (Tuscaloosa, AL) served as Alabama's eighth Poet Laureate (1995 -1999). Her books include: *Creek Captives*, *Alabama Album*, & *Silver Songs*. She also edited *These I Would Keep: Selected Poems by the Poet Laureates of Alabama*. She was named Poet of the Year in 1986 by the Alabama State Poetry Society & received the Distinguished Service Award from the Alabama Writers' Conclave in 1987.

Jeff Blake (Berea, KY) grew up in Pell City, Alabama. He attended Jacksonville State University & received degrees at Asbury College & Asbury Theological Seminary in Kentucky. For many years, he was a director with Goodwill Industries in Kentucky, Georgia & Virginia. He is presently a Major Gift Officer at Berea College in Berea, KY, a college serving the Appalachian region & beyond.

Diann Blakely (Brunswick, GA) won the Alice Fay di Castagnola Award from the Poetry Society of America for her third book, *Cities of Flesh and the Dead*. Winner of two Pushcart Prizes, she appeared in *Best American Poetry 2003*. She is co-editor of *Each Fugitive Moment*, a manuscript of responses to the poetry of the late Lynda Hull. Currently at work on a series of "duets" with Robert , she serves as a poetry editor of *Antioch Review* & also works as an arts reviewer for the Village Voice Media Group.

Ray Bradbury (Los Angeles, CA) is a noted American novelist, short-story writer, essayist, playwright, screenwriter, & poet. Acclaimed work includes *The Martian Chronicles*, *Fahrenheit 451*, & *Dandelion Wine*. He is the recipient of numerous awards including the O. Henry Memorial Award, the Benjamin Franklin Award, & the Aviation-Space Writer's Association Award.

Patricia Burchfield, (Mobile, AL) a retired mathematics educator. She earned a B. A. & an M.A. from the University of South Alabama, & holds a Doctor of Education degree from Auburn University. She writes poetry, short stories, & creative non-fiction. She recently completed three volumes of memoirs for her family.

Joanne Ramey Cage (Leeds, AL), a graduate of the University of Alabama, has won many prizes for poetry in state & national competitions & has published *Oak Mountain Echoes*, a chapbook of some of her prize-winning poems. She has written numerous short stories, & has two novels currently in the rewrite stage. She is a member of the Alabama State Poetry Society, the Oxford Shakespeare Society, the Academy of American Poets, & the Castalia Literary Club.

Bettye Kramer Cannizzo (Decatur, AL) has been published widely & has won numerous awards. *The Wind Remembers*, her first book of poems, won Book of the Year Award (2004) from the Alabama State Poetry Society. She has served on the Boards of the National League of American Women (Huntsville Branch), Alabama Writers' Conclave, & the Alabama State Poetry Society.

Jon Carter (Leeds, AL) teaches English & Creative Writing at Briarwood Christian School. He grew up as a missionary kid in Japan, attended college in Illinois & graduate school in Georgia, but now considers Alabama his home. He writes at a snail's pace between grading his students' research papers & short stories but says to expect his first novel, a political thriller in a land of pigs, in about five years.

Megan Cary (Mobile, AL) is a graphic design major in the Art Department at the University of South Alabama in Mobile. She designed the cover of *Whatever Remembers Us*.

Carol Case (Mobile, AL) is a graduate of the Creative Writing program at the University of South Alabama & a recipient of the Steve and Angelia Stokes Scholarship Award in creative writing.

Caitlin Channell (Atmore, AL) is a graduate student in Creative Writing at Portland State University in Oregon.

Mary Brobston Cleverdon (Fairhope, AL) received a B.A. in Music & English at Converse College, & an M.A. in English at the University of Alabama. She has taught at Jacksonville University & Spring Hill College. She is the author of *Questions of Form* in collaboration with the woodcuts of her husband, John. With the artist Jo Patton, she edited *Angles of Reflection*. Her poems have appeared in *Negative Capability*, *Penumbra*, & *Red Bluff Review*.

Robert Collins (Birmingham, AL) received his M.A. & Ph.D. from Ohio State University. He has received two Academy of American Poets Prizes, two Individual Artists Fellowships from the Alabama State Council on the Arts & has been nominated twice for a Pushcart Prize. He teaches American literature & creative writing at the University of Alabama, Birmingham, edits *Birmingham Poetry Review* & directs the creative writing program. His books include *The Inventor Poems, The Glass Blower* & *Occasions of Sin.*

John Curbow (Clayton, AL) has taught English & Creative Writing at Troy State University & several high schools. He has authored two collections of poetry, *The Ninth Statue* & *In Soft Wings*, as well as several other published poems, stories & essays.

Margaret G. Cutchins (1930-1999) (Auburn, AL) taught English & social studies in Virginia schools before moving to Alabama. She was published in *Elk River Review, Grandmother Earth, Octoberfest V,* & other venues. Her collection of poems, *Ladders We Climb to Who We Are*, was published in 1996 by Holly Creek Press. She garnered many awards for her poetry.

Walter Darring (Mobile, AL) is a retired English instructor from the University of South Alabama. A writer of fiction as well as poetry, he has published several books of poetry.

A.M. Davis (Mobile, AL) is completing her Master's Degree in English at the University of South Alabama.

Reese Danley-Kilgo (Huntsville, AL) writes, teaches, gardens, & plays pingpong & Scrabble with friends. Her poem about her mother in this anthology appears in her memoirs, *Scenes from a Chinaberry Childhood—Memoirs in Poetry and Prose*, still a "work in progress."

Mark Dawson (Washington, DC) has poems forthcoming in *Nimrod*, & *Measure* (where his sonnet was a finalist in the Nemerov contest). He has previously published poems in *Willow Springs, Colorado Review, North American Review, Poet & Critic, Flyway, Elk River Review, Plainsong, Antioch Review,* & others. He is a former editor of *Black Warrior Review.*

James Dickey (1923-1997) (Atlanta, GA) was one of America's foremost novelists and poets & a winner of the National Book Award for *Buckdancer's Choice.* Other honors include a Guggenheim and a Melville Cane Award, & the French Prix Médicis for his novel *Deliverance.* He read at President Carter's inauguration in 1977 & served as the Carolina Professor & Poet-in-Residence at the University of South Carolina.

Rita Dove (Charlottesville, VA) served as Poet Laureate of the U. S. & Consultant to the Library of Congress from 1993 to 1995 & as Poet Laureate of the Commonwealth of Virginia from 2004 to 2006. She has received numerous literary & academic honors, among them the 1987 Pulitzer Prize in Poetry, the 2003 Emily Couric Leadership Award, the 2001 Duke Ellington

Lifetime Achievement Award, the 1997 Sara Lee Frontrunner Award, the 1997 Barnes & Noble Writers for Writers Award, the 1996 Heinz Award in the Arts & Humanities & the 1996 National Humanities Medal. In 2006 she received the Commonwealth Award of Distinguished Service. She is Commonwealth Professor of English at the University of Virginia in Charlottesville.

Tom Drinkard (Langston, AL) has been writing poetry since he was in grade school. He was very active in writing while in college, but only restarted his poetry in the mid-eighties when he began to write about his Vietnam War experiences. His poem "The Post Office" in this anthology is part of a collection of Vietnam poems *Finding the Way Home*. He is currently busy writing technical articles & working on a novel.

Frances Durham (1889-1972) (Mobile, AL) was Mobile correspondent for *The Birmingham News*, President of the Alabama Writer's Conclave & a member of the Mobile League of American Penwomen.

Dwight Eddins (Tuscaloosa, AL) a native of Decatur, AL, was a Rhodes Scholar at Oxford University & later received his Ph.D. from Vanderbilt University. He taught Modern British & American literature at the University of Alabama for forty years. His poems have appeared in *The Sewanee Review, Prairie Schooner*, & other periodicals. He has published a portfolio of poems with collages by the artist Alvin Sella.

Deborah Ferguson (Foley, AL) received her M.A. degree from the University of South Alabama. She has received writing awards from the University of South Alabama & the Eugene Walters Writers Festival. Publications include *The Oracle* & *Margie Sound Medicine Poetry Review*. She is a teaching artist for the Alabama State Council on the Arts, the Alabama Institute for Education in the Arts & serves on the board of the Alabama Alliance for Arts Education.

John Finlay (1941—1991) (Ozark, AL) had poetry published in *The Southern Review, The Hudson Review*, & several other journals, as well as in chapbooks published by R. L. Barth Press, The Cummington Press, and the Blue Heron Press. In 1992, *Mind and Blood: The Collected Poems of John Finlay* was published by John Daniel & Company, edited by David Middleton.

Vernon Fowlkes, Jr. (Mobile, AL) has published in numerous journals & anthologies, including *Negative Capability, Willow Springs, Elk River Review, The Southern Review*, & *Literary Mobile*. His poem in this anthology is part of a three-poem series, "Beaver Meadow Triptych," based on the stories of his paternal grandmother, from the manuscript *Sleeping With*

Thunder, which is in search of a publisher.

Abby Frierson (Fairfield, PA) is a 16 year old home-schooled student who lives in Pennsylvania. She enjoys English in all its forms (reading, writing, & poetry) as well as playing soccer & spending time with friends & her three Golden Retrievers.

Maurice Gandy (Mobile, AL) teaches English at Bishop State Community as well as teaching part-time at the University of South Alabama. He is the author of *An Uncharted Inch* (Negative Capability Press) & won awards in numerous national poetry competitions.

Diane Garden (Mobile, AL) teaches creative writing to gifted students at Daphne High School in Daphne, AL. Her poems have appeared in *Jewish Spectator, Presence Africaine, MidAmerica* & other magazines. Negative Capability published her chapbook *The Hannah and Papa Poems*. In 1988, she won the Gwendolyn Brooks Poetry Award for the best poem in the Midwest Poetry Festival.

R. Garth (Athens, AL) lives & works in Athens, AL. He is currently working on a Southern "Gothic" novel.

Faye Gaston (Union Springs, AL) has been a member of the Alabama State Poetry Society since 1988. Her poetry has been published in local, state & national publications. She has published three books of poetry & given readings with visual props for civic clubs & schools. Awards include an "Outstanding Young Woman of America" in 1974, Bullock County's "Woman of the Year in 1993-94" & Hall of Fame of Robert E. Lee High School of Montgomery in 1994.

Gail Gehlken (Irvington, AL) writes poetry & creative non-fiction. She has won three Hackney Literary Awards for Poetry (2002, 2004, 2005) & seven poetry awards in Alabama State Poetry Society competitions. She has been published in *Literary Mobile* & *Potpourri*. She won first prize in the state poetry competition in the 2006 Hackney Literary Awards.

Anne George (1929-2001) (Birmingham, AL) was co-founder of Druid Press. Her poetry & prose was published extensively in journals, anthologies, & other media. *Elk River Review* first published her short story "Where Have You Gone, Shirley Temple," the characters of which went on to fame in her Southern Sisters Mystery series & to capture the Agatha Award. Her book of poetry, *Some of it is True* (1993), was nominated for a Pulitzer by the Editor of *Elk River Review*.

Charles Ghigna (Birmingham, AL), aka Father Goose, is the author of more than 30 award-winning books of poetry for children & adults from Random House, Disney, Hyperion, Knopf, Simon & Schuster, Scholastic, Abrams & other publishers. His books have been featured on ABC's "Good Morning America," selected by the Book-of-the-Month Club. His poems have appeared in *The New Yorker, Harper's, & Highlights for Children*. See the Father Goose website at FatherGoose.com.

Virginia Gilbert (Madison, AL) graduated from the Iowa Writers' Workshop & the University of Nebraska-Lincoln Ph.D. Program in Creative Writing/English. Her publications include *New Voices in American Poetry, Prairie Schooner, North American Review, & Poem*. She has received a National Endowment for the Arts grant, a Hackney Award & a 2006 Alumni Achievement Award from the University of Nebraska-Lincoln. Her books include *That Other Brightness, The Earth Above & Greatest Hits*.

Andrew Glaze (Birmingham, AL) has published eight books of poems, the first *Damned Ugly Children*, the latest *Greatest Hits*, from Pudding House. Several of his eleven plays were performed around the country. His novel *Moody's Odyssey* is currently making the rounds of major publishing houses. He is working on a second novel & a new book of poems.

Juliana Gray (Alfred NY), a native of Alabama, teaches at Auburn University. She is the author of *History in Bones & The Man Under My Skin*. She has published in *Sundog, Poetry East, Louisville Review, Formalist & Yalobusha Review*.

Theodore Haddin (Birmingham, AL) is poet, editor, reviewer, & Emeritus Professor from The University of Alabama, Birmingham, where he founded the UAB Theodore Haddin Humanities Forum. He is working on a third book of poems & has published articles on American literature. His poems have appeared in *Birmingham Poetry Review, The Chariton Review, POMPA, The Eads Bridge Review*, & various anthologies. His translation of the *Old English Seafarer* has recently appeared in *Valley Voices* (MS).

John Hafner (Mobile, AL) is a Professor of English at Spring Hill College. He has taught at Indiana University & the U. S. Military Academy at West Point. As a recipient of three Fulbright Teaching Awards he taught American Literature in Greece, Indonesia & the Philippines. His degrees are from Spring Hill College (B.S.), Marquette University (M.A.), & the University of Wisconsin-Madison (Ph.D.).

B. Kim Hagar (Athens, AL) has thought of herself as a poet & writer from the time she learned to hold a pencil. She has been published widely in such publications as *Elk River Review, Ordinary and Sacred as Blood: Alabama Women Speak,* & *Collage.: A Tribute to Steven Owen Bailey* (Negative Capability Press, 2006). She lives on the Elk River with her husband Ken and an unknown quantity of cats, birds, dogs, guinea pigs, turtles & fish.

John Halbrooks (Mobile, AL) is an Assistant Professor at the University of South Alabama. He specializes in medieval and Renaissance literature.

Dennis Hale (Notasulga, AL), a Georgia native, grew up in Opelika, AL, & earned degrees from Samford University & the New Orleans Baptist Theological Seminary before a twenty-five-year career in religious work in Spain. He has published a few poems & a satirical novel, *The Prayer Amendment,* NewSouth Books. Semi-retired, he works as a freelance Spanish interpreter/translator. Website: dennishale.com

Wade Hall (Union Springs, Al) taught at the University of Illinois, the University of Florida, & Bellarmine University in Louisville, KY. He holds degrees from Troy University, the University of Alabama, & a Ph.D. from the University of Illinois. He has authored or edited more than twenty books, including *Conecuh People: Words of Life from the Alabama Black Belt* & *The Kentucky Anthology: Two Hundred Years of Writing in the Bluegrass State.*

Mary Halliburton (Hope Hull, AL) has published in numerous publications. Her service includes: Alabama State President for the NLAPW; Treasurer, Montgomery Chapter for the NLAPW; President, 2nd VP, & Historian, Alabama Writers Conclave, President, VP & Treasurer, Montgomery Press & Authors Club; National League of American Pen Women Biennial Chair; Named Laureate Woman of Letters by the United Poets Laureates International & President, 2007 World Congress of Poets in Montgomery, AL.

Ralph Hammond (Arab, AL) was the seventh Poet Laureate of Alabama (1992 –1995). His published works began with his memories of World War II & now total 25 volumes, including 12 books & seven chapbooks of poetry. He served as Governor James "Big Jim" Folsom's press secretary & chief of staff & publicity director for the state. He is also a former mayor of Arab. Livingston University made him an honorary doctor of Letters.

Jerri Hardesty (Briarwood, AL) on poetry publishing, production, performance, promotion, preservation, & education through her nonprofit organization, New Dawn Unlimited, Inc. She & her husband organize live poetry events in Alabama & provide poetry websites, such as NewDawnUnlimited.com, PoetrySlam.net, & the local calendar page, AlabamaPoetry.com.

Michael S. Harper (Providence, RI) is University Professor & Professor of English at Brown University. He was the first Poet Laureate of the State of Rhode Island (1989-1993). He is a member of the American Academy of Arts & Sciences. He received honorary doctorate in Letters degrees from Trinity College, Coe College, Notre Dame College, Kenyon College, Rhode Island College & Washington & Jefferson University. Recent work includes *The Fret Cycle* & *Use Trouble* (forthcoming).

Kennette Harrison (San Diego, CA) has been published in numerous literary, scientific, & historical journals. She is author of *Dowsing for Light* (Elk River Review Press, 1999) which won Book of the Year from the Alabama State Poetry Society & a chapbook, *Kitchen Without Precedent* (Timberline Press, 1999).

Ava Leavell Haymon (Baton Rouge, LA) writes poems & plays. She teaches poetry writing in Louisiana during the school year, & in the summer directs a writers' & artists' retreat center in New Mexico. LSU Press published her collection *The Strict Economy of Fire* in 2004, & in 2006 published *Kitchen Heat*. She won the 2003 Louisiana Literature prize for poetry.

Dorothy Diemer Hendry (1918-2006) (Huntsville, AL) was honored by the Alabama Legislature in 2002 for her service & contribution to education. Her work includes *Something for You* (2005) & a non-fiction novel, *Looking for Jencey* (2007). Her poem "Towers of Light" was read into the U.S. Congressional Record by Rep. Bud Cramer in 2002. She chaired the Huntsville High School English Department for many years & was extremely active in state & national organizations.

Langston Hughes (1902-1967) (Harlem, NY) was one of the most important writers & thinkers of the Harlem Renaissance. An American poet, novelist, & playwright, he became one of the foremost interpreters of racial relationships in the United States.

Jay Higginbotham (Mobile, AL) prize-winning author & world traveler, has published 17 books, one of which, *Old Mobile*, won five literary awards. His Fast Train Russia was first published in the USSR in 1981 & the American edition (Dodd, Mead, 1983) was enthusiastically received in such publications as *The New Yorker, Christian Science Monitor, Kirkus Review,* & *The Library Journal*. Higginbotham's work has been translated into 27 languages, including Russian, Chinese & Arabic.

Donna Holt (Huntsville, AL) has published several poems & short stories. She received the first-place award in the Southern Literary Festival competition for her story "Rose (1989)." After attending Calhoun Community College, she graduated from Athens State College with a degree in English. She has twice been awarded the William Butler Yeats Award for creative writing, & her story "Fruit" appeared in the anthology of Alabama writers, *Alabama Bound.* Her work is frequently broadcast on WLRH public radio.

Jennifer Horne (Cottondale, AL) grew up in Arkansas & lived in Alabama since 1986. She is the editor of *Working the Dirt: An Anthology of Southern Poets* (NewSouth Books, 2003) & co-editor, with Wendy Reed, of *All Out of Faith: Southern Women and Spirituality* (University of Alabama Press, 2006). Her poetry publications include a chapbook, *Miss Betty's School of Dance* (bluestocking press, 1997), & poems in numerous journals, mostly southern.

Evelyn Hurley (Gaylesville, AL) is a retired Librarian/English teacher. She is the author of two chapbooks: *The Girl in the Velvet Rope Swing* & *The Year of Yellow Butterflies.* She has been published in *Elk River Review, The Mutant Mule, The Reach of Song, Ordinary and Sacred as Blood, Oracle, Alabama Alive* & other publications. She is past president of Alabama State Poetry Society & Alabama Writers' Conclave. She was the Alabama State Poetry Society's Poet of the Year in 2000.

Ramona L. Hyman (Huntsville, AL), poet & essayist, earned her Ph.D. degree at the University of Alabama. She serves as an assistant professor of English at Oakwood College in Huntsville. Her work has been included in magazines & anthologies such as *African American Review* & *Confirmations: An Anthology of African American Women Writers* (Marrow Press). She has served as a speaker for the Alabama Humanities Foundation.

Juanita Hendrix Holliman (Winfield, AL) works for Rebasco Decorators in Fayette, AL. Her interests include reading, writing, genealogy, arts & crafts, & serving as a Girl Scout volunteer.

Andrew Hudgins (Columbus, OH) is the author of six books of poetry. Numerous awards include the Witter Bynner Award for Poetry, the Hanes Poetry Prize and fellowships from the Bread Loaf Writers' Conference, the Ingram Merrill Foundation, and the National Endowment for the Arts. Educated at Huntingdon College, the University of Alabama, the University of Iowa, he has taught at Baylor University, the University of Cincinnati & currently teaches at Ohio State University.

Peter Huggins (Auburn, AL) poet & professor at Auburn University is the author of *Necessary Acts* (River City Publishing, 2004), *Blue Angels* (River City Publishing, 2001), *Hard Facts* (Livingston Press, 1998), *South* (Louisiana Literature Press)& a novel, *In the Company of Owls* (NewSouth Books). *Trosclair & The Alligator* (Star Bright Books, NY, 2006) was selected to appear on the PBS kids' show "Between The Lions." He received a 2006 literature fellowship from the Alabama State Council on the Arts.

J. P. Jones (Fort Payne, AL) has lived in Georgia & Alabama most of his life. The northeastern portion of Alabama is the inspiration of most of his writing. He has been in the Air Force for 11 years & is currently stationed in Northern Japan. He is studying for his B.A. in English via University of Maryland University College. Upon retirement from the military, he plans to teach high school English.

Rodney Jones (Carbondale, IL) is a professor of English at Southern Illinois University. He is the author of nine books of poetry. Numerous awards include a Guggenheim Fellowship, the Peter IB Lavan Award from the Academy of American Poets, the Jean Stein Award from the American Academy & Institute of Arts & Letters, a Southeast Booksellers Association Award, a Harper Lee Award, & the 1989 National Book Critics Circle Award.

Yvonne Kalen (Mobile, AL) has lived in Mobile since 1972. She has been engaged in numerous community activities, among them President of the Arts Patrons League, the Symphony Committee, Friends of the Library, Theatre Guild, Friends of the Ballet & Mobile Arts Council. She served as a board member for two museums & is President of the Odyssey Program at the University of South Alabama.

Willie James King (Montgomery, AL) holds an MFA from Queens University, Charlotte, & has published widely. He has been nominated for 4 Pushcart prize awards. He is humbled knowing writing isn't a means to arrogance, but a means to show humility to The Giver of gifts. He recalls that his parents passed the sign which designated: Old Cahawba, in Beloit, without ever witnessing the auction block. It was insignificant to them since they bore the residual effects of its awesome weight.

Thomas Lakeman (Magnolia Springs, AL) is the author of *The Shadow Catchers*, published by St. Martin's Press in early 2006.

Irene Latham (Birmingham, AL) serves as poetry editor for *Birmingham Arts Journal*. Her poems have appeared in various journals & in the anthology *Poems from the Big Table*. Her next book *What Came Before* is forthcoming from Negative Capability Press.

Carey Link (Huntsville, AL) has resided in several places throughout the United States & Germany. She is a Senior majoring in Psychology at The University Of Alabama in Huntsville. Her work has previously appeared in *Birmingham Arts Journal, Apathy,* & *Poem*.

Marjorie Lees Linn (1930-1979) (Collinsville, AL) grew up in dirt floor Depression-era Alabama. Between the ages of four & eleven she lived in three states, 21 cities & attended 13 grade schools. Calling herself "a migrant child," she was largely self-taught. Her literary talents placed her stories & articles in national magazines. She won numerous poetry prizes including several Hackney Awards. She worked in the Poet-In-The-Schools program. Providence Press published her *Threads from Silence* in 1980.

Penne J. Laubenthal (Athens, AL) is Professor Emeritus of English at Athens State University. Her poetry & essays have appeared in various publications including *Chocolate for a Woman's Blessing*. She regularly contributes to Sundial on WLRH Public Radio. Her article "A Humanist Looks at the Mind-Body Connection" was featured in the Journal of the Medical Association of Georgia. She offers workshops in Conflict Management & Writing for Your Life.(http://www.strategiesforsuccessinc.net/).

Hank Lazer (Tuscaloosa, AL), Associate Provost for Academic Affairs at the University of Alabama, has published 12 books of poetry, including: *The New Spirit* (Singing Horse, 2005), *Elegies & Vacations* (Salt, 2004), & *Days* (Lavender Ink, 2002). His work was nominated for a 2005 Pulitzer Prize & the 2004 Forward Prize. He & Charles Bernstein, edit the *Modern & Contemporary Poetics Series* for the University of Alabama Press. *Lyric & Spirit*, a collection of essays, will be published in 2008 by Omnidawn.

Celia Lewis (Mobile, AL) is publisher & co-editor of *Rette's Last Stand* (Tensaw Press, 2004) by Everette Maddox. She has directed poetry readings & readers' theatre series & worked as producer, actor or director in over 50 plays, reader's theatre & radio productions. She developed poetry writing workshops for fourth and fifth graders, & co-founded *The Azimuth Circle*, a high school literary magazine, at Bayside Academy in Daphne. She & her husband, Mack, own a restoration company in Mobile.

Susan Luther (Huntsville, AL) has earned degrees from LSU, UAH and Vanderbilt Universities. She has published both poetry & prose in a variety of scholarly & small-press publications.

Reilly Maginn (Daphne, AL) is the author of *Bio*. A retired surgeon who spent fifteen years in the South Pacific, he has written a multitude of award-winning short stories & teaches writing at the Eastern Shore Institute for Lifelong Learning in Fairhope, AL.

Damon Marbut (Mobile, Al) is a graduate of the University of South Alabama where he studied Creative Writing.

Barry Marks (Birmingham, AL) is an attorney. His poetry has been published in: *Folio, The Lyric, Black River Review, Legal Studies Forum, Word-Wrights!, Aura, Amaryllis* & *Calliope*. His chapbook, *There is Nothing Oppressive as a Good Man*, won the 2003 John & Miriam Morris Chapbook Competition. His poetry is featured in the recently-published anthology, *Poems from the Big Table*. He is past president of the Alabama State Poetry Society & Alabama's Poet of the Year in 1998.

Carter Martin (Huntsville, AL) writes fiction & poetry originating from his experiences in places where he has lived & worked in America, Japan, & England. He holds graduate degrees from Vanderbilt & has published literary criticism in various journals. He retired from the University of Alabama in Huntsville.

Susan Martinello (Gulf Shore, AL) is a member of the National League of American Pen Women. Her poems have appeared in *The American Muse, Grandmother Earth, Valley Planet,* & *Poem*.

Shelia Smith Mau (Cropwell, AL), currently secretary of Alabama State Poetry Society, is past president of William J. Calvert Writers, member of Alabama Writers' Conclave, & Mountain Valley Poets. Her poetry has won awards in various poetry contests. She has been published in *Soundings* & *Three O'clock at The Pines*.

Mary Brunini McArdle (Madison, AL) has a B.A. in History (English Minor) with graduate or continuing education courses in Military Strategy, English, History, Natural Science, Writing, & Art. Publication credits include: *The Villager, Mississippi Outdoors, The Roswell Literary Review,* & *Mobius*. On-line publications include: *Bewildering Stories, Combat Magazine,* & *Aphelion*.

Tom McDougle (Athens, AL) teaches in the English and Humanities Department at Athens State University. His poetry has appeared in *Barrow Street, The Literary Review, The Christian Science Monitor,* and *Elk River Review*. He is currently working on a volume of new poetry tentatively titled, *The Wit at the Staircase*.

James Mersmann (Columbiana, AL) taught American Literature & Poetry Writing at UAB for 27 years where he won numerous teaching awards including Honors Program Outstanding Faculty & university-wide Ellen Gregg Ingalls Awards. His publications include articles on contemporary poets, a literary biography of Allen Ginsberg, & *Out of the Vietnam Vortex, a Study of Poets and Poetry against the War*, as well as two books of poetry, *The Isis Poems,* & *Straying Toward Home*.

Karen Middleton (Athens, AL) is a graduate of the University of Alabama in Huntsville & a journalist, having written in the past 25 years for *Huntsville Times, Decatur Daily,* & *Athens News Courier.*

William Miller (York, PA) teaches creative writing at York College of Pennsylvania. He has published 4 collections of poetry, 12 books for children & a mystery novel. His poems & short stories have appeared in over 300 journals. He is an Alabama native & a graduate of the Alabama School of Fine Arts.

Claire Mikkelsen (Huntsville, AL) majored in English in college, did social work for ten years after that, then became a stained glass artisan.

Jessica McNealy Miles (Mobile, AL) graduated from the University of South Alabama in May 2007 where she studied Creative Writing.

Ruth Gunter Mitchell (Eastaboga, AL) is a retired English teacher & author of the novel, *Nothing But The Blood.* She writes a monthly newsletter article "Grandma's Greetings," based on her experiences as a wife, mother & grandmother. She also writes book reviews for *The Anniston Star.* Her website: http://ruthguntermitchell.com.

Shayla Mollohan (Huntsville, AL) received a B.A. degree from the University of Alabama. Her poetry has appeared in numerous publications: *Amelia, Touchstone Literary Review, Poem* & most recently, *Amaze: A Cinquain Journal.* Her first book is near completion & her work is included in a new international women's anthology to be published by Red Hen Press. She is the facilitator for Poetry-W, a sub-group within the Internet Writing Workshop.

Mary Carol Moran (Chattanooga, TN) earned her M.A. in English creative writing from UAB in 2003. Her poems have appeared in several literary magazines. *Clear Soul,* her first book of poems, was published in 2001 by Court Street Press.

John T. Morris (Cullman, AL) received his M.D. degree from Johns Hopkins University, Baltimore. He practiced internal medicine in Cullman & was an active member of the Alabama Writers' Conclave & the Alabama State Poetry Society. He is the author of *Miniature Miracle* (Honeysuckle Imprint, 1991) & *Jerome Cochran: His Life, His Works, His Legacy* with Barbara Ann McClary.

Melissa Morphew (Huntsville, TX) teaches creative writing at Sam Houston State University. She is the recipient of The Randall Jarrell International Poetry Prize, a W.B. Yeats Society Poetry Award, & an Individual

Artist's Grant in Poetry from the Tennessee Arts Commission. Her work has appeared in journals such as *The Georgia Review, Shenandoah, Prairie Schooner, & Seneca Review.* Her latest book is *Fathom* (Turning Point Press, 2006).

Carl Morton (1920-1994) (Leeds, AL), former Poet Laureate of Alabama (1983-1987), was President of the National Federation of State Poetry Societies, Inc., the Alabama State Poetry Society, & the Alabama Writers' Conclave. His books include *Desiring Stone* & *An Occasional Tyger.*

Cheryl Moyer (Montgomery, AL) received an M.P.A degree from Penn State University & is a retired FEMA inspector. She completed workshops with Robert Pinsky at Rutgers University & with Franz Wright in Provincetown, MA in 2005. Her poems have appeared in magazines in Britain, Canada & the U. S. She is Social Chairperson for the UU Church, Executive Director of Light 1 Candle, a grant writing agency for Alabama non-profit organizations & co-founder of Alabama Association of Families.

Jim Murphy (Montevallo, AL) is an Assistant Professor of English at the University of Montevallo. His poetry has appeared in The Southern *Review, Southern Humanities Review, Brooklyn Review, Painted Bride Quarterly, Cimarron Review, Fine Madness, The Alaska Quarterly Review, Puerto del Sol,* & in other journals. He serves as Director of the Montevallo Literary Festival.

Mary Murphy (Mobile, AL) is an adjunct instructor at the University of South Alabama. She was chosen to read her work at the Library of Congress in Washington DC in May 2007. She has been published in *Negative Capability* & in *Literary Mobile.*

Susan Murphy (Birmingham, AL) has been a columnist for *The Over the Mountain Journal* since 1990. Her work has appeared in *Birmingham News, Atlanta Journal/Constitution, The MacGuffin, Birmingham Arts Journal* & *Roux Magazine.* Her book, *Mad Dog Mom,* won the 1998 Small Press Award for Humor. She recently published a collection of her columns entitled *Murphy's Law: The Greatest Hits.*

Richard "Scott" Nokes (Troy, AL), originally from Indiana, became an adopted son of Alabama shortly after finishing his Ph.D. at Wayne State University in Detroit. He has been a professor of medieval literature at Troy University since 2003, & first became interested in the connections between Southern art & medieval art when he organized Troy University's "Conflict in Southern Writing" Conference. His poem in this volume honors Alabama's fine bluegrass musicians.

Helen Norris (Black Mountain, NC) served as Alabama's ninth poet laureate (1999-2003). She has two collections of poetry: *Whatever is Round* (Curbow Publications, 1994) & *Rain Pulse* (Timberline Press, 1997). She has published four novels & four short-story collections. Her honors include four O. Henry Awards, two Andrew Lytle Fiction Awards, a Pushcart Prize, & the 2000 Harper Lee Distinguished Alabama Writer Award.

Samuel Minturn Peck (1854-1938) (Tuscaloosa, AL) was Alabama's first Poet Laureate. He published seven volumes of poetry. The "grapevine" in his poem in this anthology refers to the muscadine that grows in Alabama woods. He was a former editor of the *Mobile Register*.

Phyllis H. Peck (Fairhope, AL) has been a college-level teacher for 24 years. Her poetry & professional articles have been published since 1965.

Jack Pendarvis (Atlanta, GA), a native of Bayou Le Batre, Al is the author of *The Mysterious Secret of the Valuable Treasure*.

Georgette Perry (Huntsville, AL) has published in many magazines & anthologies including *Southern Poetry Review*, *Hiram Poetry Review*, *White Heron* & *Ordinary and Sacred as Blood: Alabama Women Speak*. She is an assistant editor of *Poem*.

Lora Perry (Birmingham, AL) received a B.S. degree in secondary education from Alabama Polytechnic Institute & an M.A. degree in English from Birmingham-Southern College. She taught English in the Jefferson County Schools. She writes fiction, non-fiction, & poetry & has set some of her poems to music. Her work has appeared in *The Alalitcom* & *The Sampler*. She currently writes a column, "An Appointed Time," for the monthly publication Senior Living.

David Pratt (Kingston, Ontario, Canada) has been a factory laborer, forest fire fighter, letter carrier, teacher, & professor. Born in Britain, he spent his working life in Canada, & now divides his time between North America & Europe. His poetry & short stories have been published in many journals in Canada, the U.S., Britain, & Australia. He writes in order to defy the Second Law of Thermodynamics.

Minnie Bruce Pratt (Jersey City, NJ & Centerville, AL) is Professor of Women's Studies & Writing at Syracuse University. Author of *The Sound of One Fork*, *We Say We Love Each Other*, *Crime Against Nature*, *Walking Back Up Depot Street*, *The Money Machine*, & *The Dirt She Ate*. She received a 2005 National Endowment for the Arts Poetry Fellowship, & a Fellowship in Poetry from the New Jersey State Council on the Arts.

Kathleen Petersen (Athens, AL) has been published in *Elk River Review* & in *Collage: A Tribute to Steven Owen Bailey* (Negative Capability Press, 2006).

Marge Piercy (Wellfleet, MA) is the author of 17 novels including The New York Times Bestseller *Gone To Soldiers*; the National Bestseller *The Longings of Women* & the classic *Woman on the Edge of Time*; 17 volumes of poetry, & a critically acclaimed memoir *Sleeping with Cats*. She is the recipient of four honorary doctorates & has been a key player in major progressive political battles including the anti-Vietnam war, the women's movement, & most recently the resistance to the war in Iraq.

Michael Pollick (Decatur, AL) was born in Akron, OH. His poetry has appeared in a number of print & online publications, including the political poetry anthology *Will Work for Peace*, edited by poet/activist Brett Axel. He currently writes content for an online knowledge compendium called WiseGEEK.

Morton Prouty (1918—1992) (Florence, AL) was the sixth Poet Laureate of Alabama. He served as president of the Alabama State Poetry Society & for several years was editor of its annual publication *The Sampler*. He was a member of the American Academy of Poets & the National Federation of State Poetry Societies, Inc. His publications include: *Sparks on the Wind, Footsteps on the Mountain, The Pharisee, To a Young Mariner, The Heavens Are Telling,* & *The Edge of Time*.

Thomas Rabbitt (Lewisburg, TN) was born in Boston, MA, & educated at Harvard College, Johns Hopkins University, & the University of Iowa. Now retired, he is the former Director of the Creative Writing Program at the University of Alabama where he taught for 25 years. He has authored numerous books, most recently *American Wake: New and Selected Poems* (New South Books).

Jim Reed (Birmingham, AL) has written hundreds of stories about growing up & being in Alabama. He owns Reed Books/The Museum of Fond Memories. His website is: www.jimreedbooks.com. He is currently President of the Alabama Writers' Conclave.

Tut Riddick (Mobile, AL) received her B.A. from the University of Alabama. Actively involved with civil rights, she has worked to establish the Coleman Center for the Arts in York, AL. In addition to her work in mosaics, painting, sculpture, & photography, she has published numerous books of poetry.

Bonnie Roberts (Huntsville, AL), former Alabama State Council on the Arts Fellow & poet-in-residence, adjuncts at the University of Alabama in Huntsville. She was an NEH Fellow with Brown University in Paris; a Fellow in Verse in Dublin, & a Fulbright Scholar in Turkey. Her two volumes of poetry were nominated for the Pulitzer: *To Hide in the Light* (Elk River Review Press) & *Dances in Straw with a Two-Headed Calf* (Elk River Review Press). *To Hide in the Light* won the 1998 ASPS Book of the Year. *Dances in Straw with a Two-Headed Calf* was nominated for the Lenore Marshall Poetry Prize.

James Miller Robinson (Huntsville, AL) teaches Spanish at Huntsville High School & at the University of Alabama in Huntsville. He has recent work in *Kaleidoscope*, *Margin: Exploring Magical Realism*, *BorderSenses*, & an anthology from Saint Anthology Press: *Francis and Clare in Poetry*.

Charles Rodning, MD, (Mobile, AL) graduated from Gustavau Adolphus College magna cum laude, from the University of Rochester School of Medicine & Dentistry, & received a Ph.D. from the University of Minnesota Health Sciences Center. He is a Fellow of the International College of Surgeons & a Fellow of the American College of Surgeons. He is the recipient of numerous awards, including the Gacaner Research Award from the Minnesota Medical Foundation; the Humanism in Medicine Award, Arnold P. Gold Foundation & Healthcare Foundation of New Jersey & the Howard L. Holley Award from the Medical Association of Alabama. He has authored numerous medical articles & several books of poetry.

Julia Rowell (Durham, NC) has published poetry in *WOMB*, *Verse Libre Quarterly*, *Birmingham Arts Journal*, *MotherVerse*, & other publications including the North Carolina Poet Laureate website. She can be found online at momandapplepie.blogspot.com.

Father Abram Ryan (1834, 1836 or 1838-1886—date uncertain) (Norfolk, VA or Hagerstown, MD) was the Poet-Priest of the South. He served as a chaplain for the Confederacy & performed the funeral service for Adm. Raphael Semmes (1877). He served as editor of the Archdiocese of New Orleans official weekly newspaper, *Morning Star*, & was pastor of St. Mary's Church in Mobile, AL.

Joseph Sackett (Mobile, AL) is a retired Marine Corps officer, a former aerospace engineer, & a writer of fiction & non-fiction. He has authored six books, contributed to three others, and has penned more than 300 articles & newsletters on politics, military issues, the defense industry, & items of Southern general interest.

Patricia Sammon (Hunsville, AL) grew up in Canada. She graduated from Cornell University & completed graduate degrees at Queen's University in Kinston, Ontario. A teacher & a writer, she has received the Nelson Algren, the Cecil Hackney, and the Heekin awards. She is co-founder & co-director of the H.E. Francis Short Story Competition.

Sonia Sanchez (Philadelphia, PA) poet, activist, professor & recipient of numerous awards and honors, has authored over 16 books & edited two anthologies. A national & international lecturer on Black Culture & Literature, Women's Liberation, & Peace and Racial Justice, she has spoken at over 500 universities & colleges in the United States & has read her poetry in Africa, Cuba, England, Australia, among other international audiences. She is a contributing editor to *Black Scholar* & the *Journal of African Studies*.

Andrew Saunders (Mobile, AL) was educated in the sciences at Loyola in New Orleans. He has, for 41 years, pursued a business career unrelated to his education or his primary interests. He is President of Saunders Engine Company, a regional marine services firm.

Sue Scalf (Prattville, AL), a native of Kentucky, is a retired teacher of English & creative writing. She is widely published & has written five books of poetry: *These Brief Days*, *Devil's Wine*, *Ceremony of Names* (Druid Press) (Pulitzer nominated), *South by Candlelight* (Elk River Review Press) (Pulitzer nominated), & *What the Moon Knows* (Elk River Review Press) which won the 2003 ASPS Book of the Year.

Pat Schneider (Amherst, MA), poet, playwright, librettist, workshop & retreat leader, speaker & teacher as well as Founder & Director Emeritus of Amherst Writers & Artists, is the author of nine books, including *Writing Alone & With Others* from Oxford University Press.

Kate Seawell (Mobile, AL) received a B.A. in Russian literature & English literature from Cornell University where she studied creative writing with Alison Lurie & Baxter Hathaway. She then became a visual artist & has pursued that career for many years. After earning a B.F.A in painting from the University of South Alabama & an M.A. in Art from Spring Hill College, she currently teaches at the University of South Alabama as an adjunct instructor in the Department of Visual Arts.

Thomi Sharpe (Saraland, AL) is a family physician in Prichard, AL. She currently lives on the Alabama Delta at Bayou Sara. This is her first poetry publication.

Jim Simmerman (1952-2006) (Flagstaff, AZ) was Regents Professor of English at Northern Arizona University in Flagstaff. He is the author of *Home* (Dragon Gate, Inc., 1983), chosen by Raymond Carver as a Pushcart "Writer's Choice" Selection; *Once Out of Nature* (The Galileo Press, Ltd., 1989), a "Best of the Small Presses" feature at the Frankfurt Book Fair; *Moon Go Away, I Don't Love You No More* (Miami U. Press, 1994); *Kingdom Come* (Miami U. Press, 1999); and *American Children* (Boa Editions, 2005).

Christopher Singleton (Semmes, AL) is an undergraduate student of creative writing at the University of South Alabama. After graduation, he aspires to attend law school.

Vivian Smallwood (Chickasaw, AL) was born in Vinegar Bend, AL. She lived most of her life in Chickasaw, AL. She is the author of *Window to the South* & *Finding No Mouse There.*

Eric D. Smith (New Market, AL) is Assistant Professor of English at the University of Alabama in Huntsville, where he specializes in Modern British & Postcolonial literatures.

R. T. Smith (Rockbridge County, VA) edits *Shenandoah: The Washington & Lee University Review.* His poetry books include *The Hollow Log Lounge* (University of Illinois Press), *Brightwood* (LSU Press), *Messenger, Split the Lark: Selected Poems, Trespasser, Hunter-Gatherer, The Cardinal Heart,* & *From the High Dive. Trespasser* & *The Cardinal Heart* received Pulitzer Prize nominations.

Betty Spence (Mobile, AL) earned a B.A. degree in English in 1978 from the University of South Alabama where she also pursued graduate studies. She has published poems in a wide range of publications. She is a former *Mobile Press Register* correspondent, photographer,& columnist. She is the author of a collection of poetry *Pinned-on Wings* (Timberline Press, 2004).

Glenda Richmond Slater (Fairhope, AL), received her M.A. from University of Alabama & Ph.D. from University of Cincinnati. She has published light verse, serious verse, children's poems, a children's play, as well as several articles on communication.

Julie Suk (Charlotte, NC) attended Stephens College & the University of Alabama. She is the author of *The Dark Takes Aim* (Autumn House Press); *The Angel of Obsession; Heartwood* ; & *The Medicine Woman* . She co-edited *Bear Crossings: An Anthology of North American Poets* with Anne Newman & Nancy Cooke Stone. Her poems have appeared in such journals as *Georgia Review, Shenandoah,* & *Poetry* which awarded her the Bess Hokin Award.

Catherine Swender (Mobile, AL) is originally from Michigan, where she lived until moving to Mobile in 2004. She received her Ph.D. from Michigan State University & currently works as an Assistant Professor of English at Spring Hill College. Her specialties include poetry, nineteenth-century British literature & gothic fiction. In addition to writing poetry, she enjoys playing the piano & gardening.

Peggy Teel (Birmingham, AL) is the author of *God and Grandma, Pottery Lessons,* & *Know Alabama* (Phroughdyrie Press, 2006).

Seth Tanner (Talladega, AL) has been published in *Birmingham Random Acts of Art !, Birmingham Arts Journal,* & *Poem.* He is currently pursuing his M.A. in Liberal Studies at Jacksonville State University with plans to teach at the community college level.

Marilyn Tarvin (Toney, AL) is a retired engineer who now has the time to explore her right brain. She has been published in the Limestone Dust Poetry Festival 2006 Anthology. She is currently working on a collection of poems & a mystery novel.

Donna Jean Tennis (Montgomery, AL) is past president of Alabama Writers' Conclave, Alabama State Association of NLAPW, Montgomery Creative Writers, & is the perennial newsletter/anthology editor for the Alabama State Poetry Society. A contest "junkie" (more than 100 first place awards), her poetry & prose have been published in numerous journals, magazines, & anthologies. Her first poetry collection *Love on Wry* won the Alabama State Poetry Society's 1996 Book of the Year.

Jeanie Thompson (Montgomery, AL), executive director of the Alabama Writers' Forum, founded the *Black Warrior Review.* She authored *How To Enter the River, Witness,* & *White for Harvest: New & Selected Poems,* & co-edited *The Remembered Gate: Memoirs by Alabama Writers.* Fellowships were received from the Louisiana Arts Council & the Alabama State Council on the Arts. She teaches poetry in the Spalding University Brief Residency MFA Writing Program (Louisville, KY).

Kathleen Thompson (Birmingham, AL), is a University of Alabama graduate & a former teacher of English & Creative Writing. She holds an M.F.A from Spalding University. Recent poems have appeared in *Birmingham Poetry Review, Oracle,* & *Thicket.* Her published chapbook of poetry is *Searching for Ambergris.* A story "Living like the Lilies" is included in *Climbing Mt. Cheaha: Emerging Alabama Writers.* She is a 2007-2008

Speakers Bureau "Road Scholar" of the Alabama Humanities Foundation.

Teresa K. Thorne (Springville, AL) enjoys a second career as the executive director of City Action Partnership (CAP) after retiring as a Birmingham police captain. Her writing interests include short stories, novels, screenplays, & poetry.

Margaret J. Vann (Huntsville, AL) has been writing since her graduate poetry class with Dr. August Mason at the University of Alabama. Her poems have been published in small magazines, including *Muse, The Scribbler, Red Mountain Rendezvous, Poem,* & *The Sampler*. She has been editor of the *Historic Huntsville Quarterly,* a preservation publication.

Margaret (Maggi) Britton Vaughn (Bell Buckle, TN), is Poet Laureate of Tennessee. Her poetry collections include: *Grand Ole Saturday Nights, Light in the Kitchen Window, Kin, Acres that Grow Stones,* & *America Showing Her Colors in Black and White*. She is also a playwright & songwriter.

Doris Gabel Welch (Athens, AL), has an M.A. in Art Education & has taught kindergarten through university level classes. She is a published writer, Fulbright scholar & an exhibiting artist in museum shows & galleries. She won the purchase award for her landscape painting in the Wonders of Alabama Art in Birmingham.

Jason R. Walker (New York, NY) is a graduate student in the Music Business program at New York University. He is a sound designer & photographer whose photographs are featured on the cover of *Whatever Remembers Us*.

Frank X Walker (Cincinnati, OH) is the author of *Affrilachia*. His work has appeared in numerous journals & anthologies.

Claiborne Schley Walsh (Daphne, AL) is a writer, artist, sculptor, & educator. She is multi-published, a winner of many poetry competitions & has been featured in more than 10 states & two continents. She has given workshops on creative thinking & poetry writing.

Eugene Walter (1921-1998), (Mobile, AL) a Mobile icon & Renaissance man, was an advisory editor of *Negative Capability, Botteghe Oscure in Rome,* & a founder of *The Paris Review*. He is the author of *The Untidy Pilgrim, American Cooking: Southern Style*, novels, & numerous short stories.

Rob Whitaker (Birmingham, AL), is a student at Briarwood Christian School who enjoys wandering through the deciduous forests of Alabama.

Patti White (Tuscaloosa, AL) teaches creative writing at the University of Alabama. Her publications include: *Arts Indiana*; *Mississippi Review, Atlanta Review, Iowa Review,* & *North American Review.* She is the recipient of a MacGuffin National Poet Hunt Award & The Anhinga Prize for Poetry . *Tackle Box,* a poetry collection, was published by Anhinga Press. An award-winning festival-short film of the title poem was released in 2003 (www.tackleboxthemovie.com). *Yellow Jackets,* was published by Anhinga Press in 2007.

Isabelle Whitman (New Orleans, LA) is a graduate of the University of South Alabama. She currently lives and works in New Orleans.

Joseph Whitten (Odenville, AL) was born in Bryant, AL, on Sand Mountain. He is author of *Mulled Memories* (Mulberry River Press). He was the Alabama State Poetry Society's Poet of the Year in 2002. After teaching for 39 years, he retired in 2000 & has enjoyed writing poetry & collecting death notices from old St. Clair County, AL, newspapers.

Nancy Compton Williams (Huntsville, AL), a retired teacher, has had some 100 poems published in journals such as *Theology Today, Sacred Journey,* & *Hiram Poetry Review.* Her first book of poetry is entitled *Stillness Walks on Water.* She serves on the editorial board of *Poem.*

Miller Williams (Fayetteville, AR) has published thirty-three books. His work has represented the U. S. State Department on reading & lecture tours throughout Latin America, Europe, & the Middle & Far East. He has served as Visiting Professor of U.S. Literature at the University of Chile, & as a Fulbright Professor of American Studies at the National University of Mexico. He was the inaugural poet for the second inauguration of President Bill Clinton. He retired in 2003 from the position of University Professor of English & Foreign Languages at the University of Arkansas.

William J. Wilson (Huntsville, AL) is a writer of light & serious verse as well as short stories (Horror & Sci Fi), & has appeared in such diverse media as *The Saturday Evening Post, The Progressive Farmer, New York Magazine, Twilight Zone Magazine, The Washington Post, Poem* & other literary magazines. He retired from UNISYS in 1992 & since has become a prize-winning mosaic artist.

Jamie Yerby (Mobile, AL) graduated from the University of South Alabama with a double major in Theatre Arts & English with a concentration in Creative Writing.

Jake Adam York (Denver, CO) was reared in northeast Alabama. He teaches creative writing & poetics at the University of Colorado at Denver. His work has appeared in *The Southern Review, The Greensboro Review, Gulf Coast, Crab Orchard Review, Shenandoah, & Poetry Daily.* He is the author of *Murder Ballads.*

C.W. Zoan (Bayou La Batre, AL), author of 13 books of poetry, is the owner of Balm Coast Marine Manufacturers.

Editors, Whatever Remembers Us

Sue Brannan Walker

is the Poet Laureate of Alabama and Chair of the English Department at the University of South Alabama. She is the author of six books of poetry, has edited several anthologies, and has published critical articles on James Dickey, Flannery O'Connor, and Marge Piercy. She is the publisher of Negative Capability Press and lives in Mobile, AL.

J. William Chambers

is poet, writer, critic, and author of *Camellias in Autumn* (1989, Honeysuckle Imprint), *A Taste of Wine and Gentian* (2000, Negative Capability Press). He is editor of and contributor to *Collage: A Tribute to Steven Owen Bailey* (2006, Negative Capability Press). His poetry, reviews, and essays have been widely published in numerous journals, magazines, and other media. He was founding editor and publisher of *Elk River Review* (1990 - 1999). He was awarded the Distinguished Alumnus Award from Athens State University in 1987. He lives in Athens, AL.